Evil
How our culture is going off the rails

Evil

How our culture is going off the rails

by

Notker Wolf
Leo G. Linder

Translated by
Gerlinde Büchinger-Schmid

Edited by
Sue Bollans

DK
PRINTWORLD
Publishers of Indian Traditions

Cataloging in Publication Data — DK
[Courtesy: D.K. Agencies (P) Ltd. <docinfo@dkagencies.com>]

Wolf, Notker, author.
[Böse. English]
Evil : how our culture is going off the rails / by Notker Wolf,
Leo G. Linder ; translated by Gerlinde Büchinger-Schmid ;
edited by Sue Bollans.
pages cm
Translated from German.
ISBN 9788124608722

1. Sin, Mortal. 2. Christian ethics. I. Linder, Leo G., 1948-
author. II. Büchinger-Schmid, Gerlinde, translator. III.
Bollans, Sue, editor. IV. Title.

BV4626.W65 2016   DDC 241.3   23

Original title: Das Böse. Wie unsere Kultur aus den Fugen gerät
by Notker Wolf and Leo G. Linder
© 2015 by Gütersloher Verlagshaus, Gütersloh/München
a division of Verlagsgruppe Random House GmbH, München, Germany

ISBN: 978-81-246-0872-2
First English translation published in India in 2016
© Gerlinde Büchinger-Schmid

Printed and published by:
D.K. Printworld (P) Ltd.
Regd. Office: Vedaśrī, F-395, Sudarshan Park
(Metro Station: Ramesh Nagar), New Delhi – 110 015
Phones: (011) 2545 3975, 2546 6019
e-mail: indology@dkprintworld.com
Website: www.dkprintworld.com

Content

1

An unwanted but persistent guest

God gives up. He loses patience and all he can think of doing is "blot out from the earth the human beings I have created." How? By a flood: "I am going to destroy them along with the earth." And why? Because "the wickedness of humankind was great in the earth and that every inclination of the thoughts of their hearts was only evil," for "the earth was corrupt in God's sights depraved and the earth was filled with violence," and therefore he "is sorry that I have made them." So he has it rain for forty days and forty nights "and the waters swelled and increased greatly on the earth that all high mountains under the whole heaven were covered. And all flesh died that moved on the earth ... Everything on the dry land in whose nostrils was the breath of life died." Except Noah, the only righteous man.

The flood — what is it but the response of someone who is totally at a loss? At a loss and profoundly disappointed in a human race that will not listen to reason, willfully conspires to bring about its own end, and spreads like putrefaction over the earth. But the God of the Bible is not the only one who is disappointed. The highest God of the Greeks is similarly at a loss.

"Zeus, the ruler of the world, received bad news about the iniquities of the people. He therefore decided to wander the earth in human form. But everywhere he found the truth even worse than the rumor." He is also aghast. On his return to Olympia he consults with the gods and decides to destroy the nefarious human race: How? With "huge cloudbursts and endless floods."

The result is the same as it was in the first case. Only a single human couple survives, Deucalion and Pyrrha, "both blameless and worshippers of the deity." Although mankind continues to exist after this and begins afresh after the massive flood, the basic problem remains unchanged — people are as they are, they remain as they were and even the righteous Noah has nothing better to do after his rescue than indulge in an orgy of drinking. God is the only one who comes to his senses. Disillusioned, he comes to terms with the incorrigibility of human beings "because the imagination of man's heart is evil from his youth" and makes peace with the rabble. "That never again shall all flesh be cut off, as I have done." The conclusion reached by Zeus is not revealed in the Greek myth. But he too makes no further attempt to get to the root of the problem.

It is hopeless. Human beings are fundamentally evil, rotten to the core and God himself is at a loss. "There is nothing more appalling than man, for he is capable of anything," said the Greek tragedian Sophocles long ago, and a subsequent thinker likened people to beasts, as dangerous to their own kind as wolves. If any lesson can be drawn from the history of mankind then it is this: abandon all hope . . .

Is this judgement too harsh? Isn't it unfair? One thing we do have to admit: we are not unfamiliar with this feeling of helplessness in the face of evil. We have no need to study court records, we only have to look at history books or open our ears to the conversation at the next table in canteens or cafés — cries of war, revenge, and pain echo a thousandfold down all the ages of mankind and reverberate a thousandfold in complaints about everyday meanness perpetrated by disloyal friends, inconsiderate neighbors, malevolent relatives, outrageous colleagues, and self-important superiors. Evil seems to bubble up from inexhaustible sources, and where it prevails or even when it is merely talked about it generates reactions ranging from headshaking to disbelief and dismay. How can anyone be or act like that, how can anyone simulate, err, get carried away or offend in this way? Whether the evil we encounter is in the shape of a rather harmless office intrigue or the repugnant figure of a child abuser, we can never understand it. It always leaves us speechless. It is as if evil were a sinister intruder of mysterious origin that has nothing to do with us and basically has no place in this world.

But is evil then part of us? Is it not actually alien to us? Downright alien?

That would be a bold claim. Who could deny that it is the privilege of man to be evil? Everything else that could otherwise cause us trouble, threaten us, put us in a state of panic or in fear of our lives — wild animals, accidents, natural disasters — is classified as deplorable happenstance, misfortune, and tragedy. It would never occur to us to impute malice to an earthquake or a watchdog that bites for the simple reason that we can't attribute intention to an animal or natural disasters. But evil involves reason, free will, responsibility, which are the things that characterize human beings and distinguish them from the rest of creation. How should evil then be unknown to them?

But nevertheless . . .

Nevertheless we most definitely want nothing to do with it. Nevertheless we understand the indignation of the old lady who said to me when the topic of confession came up, "I really don't know what I would have to confess! As far as I can remember I haven't done anything wrong." And in fact, most of us when we look inside ourselves would notice nothing even remotely reminiscent of malice. Even the convicted serial offender will say of himself I'm not a bad person. Is that mere self-deception? Mere self-pity? Or can we confirm this feeling of getting entangled in something, finding ourselves on a slippery slope and suddenly no longer understanding ourselves? Doesn't evil seem to come out of the blue or rather out of a threateningly black sky, as if it existed outside of this order, this world order, in another dimension, separated from us by an abyss, whereby we take it for granted that we are part of this order — or at least want nothing more than to be part of it?

At this point I begin to suspect God might have been mistaken when he directed his anger against the people. Had he really seriously examined the situation? I realize that here we are trying to follow the train of thought of the person who wrote down the story of the flood — understanding the mind of God is beyond us.

But let's go back to the original story, let's follow the logic of this God who sent the flood. Does this decision neglect the fact that human beings equally find evil a curse? That they also suffer and see in evil an unwanted but persistent guest — like a parasite that has chosen people as its host. Should God not have sought allies in human beings — and would he not have found them? At any rate the flood changed nothing — it was a failure, good only as an example of the ineradicability of evil. Because, as in a horror movie, it survives aboard the ark, rooted in the soul of the righteous Noah and breaks out again as life on earth continues. Everything remains the same. God should have probably selected a different starting point in his battle against evil. But where should this have been?

In the system for example — to move from the flood to the present day. In the perfidious political system or unjust social conditions. According to one diagnosis, poverty is the fundamental evil and it has increasingly prevailed in recent decades. Moral behavior is only possible on a full stomach, which is why a well-fed person is always more agreeable than a hungry one and a wealthy person fundamentally more peaceful than a needy one. Such views are popular in leftist circles. This suggests that the individual is not altogether morally sound and there are in fact enough examples of the way the conscience adapts to the prevailing evil conditions or gives up entirely in the face of a chain of unfortunate events, of the way chance and unfortunate constellations bring our best intentions to naught.

Others see our basic biological constitution as the source of evil. They consider human behavior to be caused by a kind of automatic chemical reaction in the human nervous system center before the person is conscious of it. Or they say the genes are egoistic, which unfortunately removes all possibility of choice from us. According to this we are completely helpless, as equally at the mercy of our biological constitution as of the political and social conditions in the above case — remote control inevitably comes to mind. In whatever system we locate the cause of evil, whether in the political, the social or the biological system, it is always beyond our reach, so we can finally feel understood: yes, evil is a result of the constraints of the environment into which we are born or in which we have placed ourselves, as unpredictable as a workplace accident and outside our control.

Maybe God should have begun here? With society, politics, the functioning of the human brain?

There are many angles from which we could look at this subject. Let us hold fast to our first impression before we examine one aspect after the other: Evil irritates. No one in their right mind wants it and yet it prevails. It takes on a disturbing life of its own and its dominance seems unnatural to us — in Biblical terms a condition never intended by God. It overshadows the existence of the individual and hovers like a storm front over the life of the world's people — trifling incidences give rise to slaughter as if developments were blindly following a diabolical logic and when a small group of people take up their guns, possibly with honorable motives, it's not long before an entire country is at war with itself. Tremendous energies come into play and one thing can already be said: whatever it is, wherever it comes from, evil is uncanny. And one must add, like all uncanny things, it has an irresistible fascination.

It occupies and excites us. What would any artistic production, literature, painting, theatre, movie be without evil, the dark side of man, his abyss? And of course the scandal of evil runs right through the Bible almost from the first to the last page, from the paradise story to the Apocalypse. But what in fact is it? This evil that even a flood could not sweep away . . .

2

The boy with the spider

I think about evil in the same way as Saint Augustine thought about
the phenomenon of time. As long as I do not concern myself with it,
I have a clear idea of it. But the more closely I look at it, the more
uncertain I become. The picture I have of evil dissolves, literally
shatters into the numerous aspects in which it presents itself in
everyday life, ranging from cold indifference to the misfortune
of strangers and the poisoning effect of jealousy to the horror of
battlefields, and I ask myself whether its essence can be determined
at all. Or must we accept that we can narrow it down but never
grasp it?

And then it occurs to me that painters have tried to do this.
Over and over again. They had no other choice. They had to make
visible in concentrated form — combine in single picture — all the
clever speculations with which poets, philosophers, and theologians
fill books. In an attempt to determine the nature of evil I will thus
first consult the painters of the Middle Ages and see what forms of
representation they found for absolute good and absolute evil. In
other words what characteristics they gave to God in their paintings
and what they gave to the devil.

You are naturally rather left to your own devices if you want to
make the invisible visible. God is spirit and so is the devil, and the
Bible doesn't provide useful statements for painters about either
of them. It assigns one to the sphere of light and the other to the
sphere of darkness — and that's all it tells us. It's an arbitrary act
of the artist to give God or the devil a human or semi-human form
complete with facial features and gestures, but it's very helpful for

us. We can now read the characteristics of absolute good (as well as absolute evil) from a facial expression or a particular posture and for this we require no more than a little knowledge of human nature.

First God.

The medieval depictions of God are remarkably uniform. Whether you see the attributes of the wise ruler, the benevolent father, the serene old man or the spiritual philosopher in the face of God, this countenance doesn't reflect any emotion. It's all earnestness, sovereign calm, and inscrutability. It also looks intently at the observer. God is rarely shown from the side, he almost always looks at us face on — *he* looks at us and *we* look back at him and we absorb his tranquility. This is the essence of it. In the picture of the serene wise man we are intended to recognize absolute good. This is how a person would look at us with whom everything is in order.

And now the devil.

What strikes us first is that no one devil is like another. Here the artistic imagination knows no limits and the painters go into the most bizarre detail. However, the devil is always deformed, is part man and part animal with a distorted, grotesque physiognomy that clearly reflects emotions such as mockery, ridicule, cunning or lust, and eyes that glint evilly with demonic triumph. In addition, the devil is depicted in action. He's almost always doing something, poking around, pulling, stirring up, snaring, all in all the exact opposite of someone who is well-balanced and trustworthy. Not a person who could look you in the eye. And there's something else: The devil seems to feel comfortable with what he's doing. He exudes a scornful satisfaction, and sometimes seems to be having infantile fun. This image of an irrational troublemaker is intended to suggest absolute evil. This is the effect a person with whom nothing is right would have on us.

It's clear that these pictures are not mere artistic whims. They reflect a long tradition of thought, an analysis of good and evil which goes back to ancient times. They're representative and well-founded and therefore all the more revealing. What message do they contain? Without reading any moral qualities into these images, I would say that the good embodied in the image of God represents humanity purified of all passions, steadfast, at peace with itself, unimpressionable, unassailable, and thus trustworthy. The evil embodied in the devil, however, is inhumanity churned up by passion, unsettled, restless, bestially irrational, tense, driven, and at the same time self-satisfied and thus terrifying. In sum, we could perhaps say that good is represented as unassailable, sovereign self-control, evil as instinct-driven instability.

This is at any rate a start, and we can immediately see there is something in it. It's correct that we think more about what we are doing when we do good than when we do evil (unless we are professional gangsters or totalitarian rulers). When as children we shared our orange with a classmate in the playground, or when we later made a donation for disaster victims somewhere in the world, then we always did this with aforethought based on certain considerations or well-founded compassion. The hateful and hurtful usually overcomes us unexpectedly, we get a sudden urge, are irresistibly driven and often only realize what we've done when we come to our senses. A little story comes to my mind, which at first seems harmless.

A ten-year-old boy confessed to me that he had chased his little sister upstairs with a spider. I had to smile. "It's not tragic," I said to the repentant sinner, "It was just a stupid prank . . ." But the boy shook his head vigorously. "No," he said, "I know how scared my sister is of spiders. And I enjoyed frightening her." Then I understood. He had discovered the pleasure of evil and was horrified at himself.

It is indeed frightening, this uncanny desire for torturing and lambasting another person. "I enjoyed frightening my sister . . ." — as if a previously hidden cellar door had opened and a new, strange breath of temptation had wafted out of the darkness. Frightening, but at the same time . . .

Now, if the boy had behaved properly, picked up the spider carefully and put it outside, he would have had nothing to relate, nor would his sister. But because he had succumbed to temptation and waved the nasty animal in front of his horrified sister's face, the encounter with the spider became a little story that was upsetting for both of them but actually instructive for the boy. What I'm trying to point out is something that is easily overlooked. Evil has not only a moral but also a dramatic dimension.

Both aspects are inseparably interwoven, and both affect the evaluation of an evil deed — one person will be merely repelled, another will see in it the material for a story. However, this is not everything. The dramatic dimension may stimulate not only the observer, but also the perpetrator. I would like to give as an example one of the most spectacular criminal cases of the last century, that of the serial killer Peter Kürten, known at the time as the "Vampire of Düsseldorf."

In 1929, an eight-year-old girl was found murdered in Düsseldorf and for 16 months new murders and attempted murders occurred every few weeks. The victims were with a single exception young women and girls, killed with a hatchet, slain with a hammer or stabbed to death with scissors. When Peter Kürten was arrested in 1931 after nine murders and 32 attempted murders, the case attracted worldwide attention.

The circumstances of the individual murders are horrifying but this is not the point I want to make here. "I had the strong desire to kill a person," Kürten said during his interrogation, thus alluding to the sexual satisfaction he derived from the sight of flowing blood. What I find significant is that Kürten placed great value on the dramatic effect of his deeds. On the morning after a murder, he mingled with the crowd come to gawp at the scene, not just in order to enjoy to the full the reactions of his public, but above all to check whether he had created as much horror as he desired and expected. He confessed when he was interrogated that after every crime, "I imagined the effect that this murder would have on Düsseldorf's population," — whereby it could have barely escaped him either that he was gradually attracting worldwide attention.

In other words, the abominable was to some extent a drama deliberately staged by Kürten; his ambition was to generate the greatest possible amount of shock. This motive became even more prominent after he was arrested, when he subjected the interrogating police officers to an endless narrative. With his razor-sharp memory he confessed incessantly, giving all the grisly details, and even confessed acts he had never committed. "I thought you liked it when I confessed to a lot of crimes," he said in apology for his false statements. What this means is that Kürten felt comfortable in the role of a monster. He deliberately exploited the dramatic capital of a criminal life. With the result that people from all over the world flocked to the court hearing — thirsting for revenge but also eager for more sensational revelations. When the judgment was announced, his narrative power flowed into numerous letters written to his surviving victims before he was executed by guillotine in 1931.

Incidentally the movie director Fritz Lang based his famous movie "M — a city looks for a murderer" on this case, which I feel is in tune with the logic behind this series of murders. Kürten would certainly have understood the movie as the crowning achievement of his "life's work."

Presumably it's not uncommon for a serial killer not to take morality into consideration; Kürten, in any case, by his own account felt entitled to do what he did. However, what seems unusual here is that a murderer acted in full awareness of the dramatic dimension of evil and staged his life like a gruesome story, at least during the period of his crimes, or acted like the producer of a shocking play. In addition to the sexual satisfaction at the moment of killing, this aspect seems to have given him the greatest satisfaction.

What does this case imply for our search for the nature of evil? Let's return to the medieval depictions of God and the devil. If we now also now judge them by their dramatic effect, we make another, rather disturbing discovery.

The God of the painters — you cannot say otherwise — is boring. He has no surprises up his sleeve. He's always the same old man, impassive, remote from everything going on around him and very far from arousing our curiosity. We glance at him and we are in the picture. The reason why our eyes scan the wall paintings and stained glass windows of a church is much more likely to be the devil. And there we take a good look. He's ugly, repugnant, horrible. He lurks with a wicked grin in a window, the spooky effect increased by the bluish light that is cast from outside on his crouching body, or he jumps out of a wall niche as a scaly monster. In a word, you can experience something with the devil. He fascinates and excites us as only evil can, and the lukewarm, pleasant feeling we have for what is good comes nowhere near this. Painting thus confirms what we've already suspected after the story of the boy and the spider or the case of Peter Kürten: for our nervous system evil is just what we were waiting for, and by dramatic standards highly superior to what is good.

And suddenly it's as if we were trying to get a foothold on a steep scree slope. Evil is ambiguous. It is not just evil. It changes like the color of certain materials in different lights. However repugnant we may find it morally, we find it extraordinarily attractive from a dramatic point of view. In addition, whatever our attitude, whether we respond with aversion or succumb to its attraction, it puts us in a state of excitement, which good rarely does. We know this of course as TV viewers, moviegoers, or readers of thrillers. Few are however aware of the extent of our sensitivity to the shock waves of evil. Amazingly, we register the shocks triggered by evil even over long distances, as if they had no limits in time or space.

It doesn't even need to affect us personally, we don't even have to be witnesses — our moral judgment covers the whole world and evil doesn't lose any of its destructive power even when it only reaches us as news from a remote corner of the earth. Yes, even the most distant past is detected by our moral radar. Even atrocities that happened long ago such as the manhunts of slavers in Africa or the massacre of the Thirty Years' War can still make us indignant. They act on us as if the memory of them would never fade, as if the energies of every evil deed were stored somewhere, as if these deeds were waiting for us to acknowledge them with fear, indignation or disgust after thousands of years. The good deeds of the past receive at most our gracious consent. The good happening elsewhere in the world doesn't disturb our peace of mind. But evil affects us regardless of how long ago or far away a deed was done. It takes root in our soul and finds a much more powerful reverberation there than all the good that is also incessantly happening and has ever happened on our planet.

It's probably our fascination with evil that so easily gives it power over our thoughts and feelings. We're involuntarily put in a state of concentrated excitement mixed with a substantial portion of pleasure. For Sigmund Freud is wrong when he says human beings fear nothing more than excitement. The truth is rather that they usually fear nothing more than the absence of excitement. Evil serves this need for excitement extremely well, it fascinates us, and as a final example, I would like to tell the story of a dramatic surrender to the fascination of evil. You can find it in the autobiographical *Confessions* of St. Augustine (354–430).

His boyhood friend Alipius, Augustine recounts, had become a staunch opponent of the gladiator fights after his conversion to Christianity. One day, however an acquaintance applied gentle force to get him to the amphitheater. We're familiar with this kind of persuasion: don't make such a fuss, come with me, people say in such situations, and who wants to be a spoilsport? So although Alipius abhorred bloodshed, he couldn't extricate himself and swore to endure the gruesome spectacle with closed eyes. "Would to God he had stopped his ears too," Augustine continues, "for at a certain point in the fight, a mighty cry from all the people made him so curious that he opened his eyes as if prepared to despise and be superior what he saw. And then his soul was pierced with a wound deeper than the gladiator's ... For as soon as he saw the blood he was seized with a wild craving and didn't turn away but fixed his eyes on the spectacle, drank in all the fury and was intoxicated with cruel pleasure in the bloody savagery ... Nor was he now the man he came in as but one of the multitude with which he mingled ..."

From then on, we read, Alipius was addicted to gladiator games.

You can sense almost physically the force of the temptation to which poor Alipius succumbs in this story. It surges towards him, knocks him over, and carries him off. When he opens his eyes, all is lost. The transformation from an opponent to a fanatic supporter of the cruel games happens in a single moment as if he's been touched by a magic wand. Good has to work much harder with us. Tremendous forces must be at work when absolute repudiation can change from one moment to the next into feverish enthusiasm. What are these forces? Augustine at least gives us some pointers, speaking of lust, wantonness, and drunkenness. He diagnoses complete loss of control. And this, although on a much smaller scale, is exactly what the boy with the spider discovered in himself. This is exactly what Peter Kürten felt at the sight of flowing blood. And it seems that the devils of the medieval painters are showing similar characteristics. The failure of reason, intractable instability, and loss of control.

Have we then discovered the most important thing about evil? Can it be explained by the irruption of the irrational into the ordered world of reason? Are we overwhelmed by the irresistible power of lust and desire? However, can't the same thing be said about love? Doesn't something similar apply to all forms of enthusiasm? And is good on the other hand really only the product of self-control, the result of sensible consideration and rational deliberation? Must you be a moral philosopher or ascetic in order to halfway succeed at resisting? In this case, God who sent the flood would have been right: in the earthly turmoil that met his eye, moral philosophers and ascetics would have been a rarity, the absolute exception. And finally, even if we have to rate the entertainment value of evil as much greater than that of good, don't we ultimately always want good to be victorious in spite of all our fascination with what's gruesome?

3

The power of evil

It is my guess that most of us would be upset by a movie that ended with the victory of evil. How many of us would accept without a murmur an ending where the traitor, the miser, the jealous neurotic or the cold-hearted killer was victorious instead of getting what he or she deserved. I know such plays and movies do exist, but if we are honest, they go against the grain. We don't want to go home with the image of the maliciously grinning mafioso. Even when it initially looks as if evil is going to win, we start to feel discomforted and our moral nervous system reacts with growing nausea. And if evil really does triumph we feel properly snubbed. No, we insist on the victory of good.

Of course at the beginning everything is allowed to go wrong. Even go seriously wrong and shake the foundations of our ideal world. Evil can do its worst, there can be a few repulsive characters and a few corpses — but at the last moment the kidnapper must be felled by a bullet and his victim must weep, speechless with happiness. Our ideal is a catastrophe with a happy ending, of that there is no doubt.

This also makes me think of the remarkable fact that it is the predators in the zoo that draw the largest numbers of people. Herbivores are usually of less interest, they are harmless, they are peaceful, and, like the God of the painters, you only have to glance at them to know what they are all about. The attraction is the predators' enclosure — but woe betide any hyena that dares to pursue its favorite activity and tear a live animal to pieces in front of everyone! We want to spare ourselves *that* scene, our nerves are not actually that strong after all. Terrible, dangerous things are bearable and even most welcome only in a defused form, subdued and harnessed, like a halfway well-behaved zoo lion or an episode of a crime series on television.

Once again we encounter the phenomenon of fascination. Evidently we human beings want to experience both the proximity of evil and the triumph of good, at least when it doesn't affect us and we are merely the audience. Can the flood of crime, war and disaster movies from Hollywood and TV companies perhaps be explained by the fact that as spectators we also see both the villain and the innocent party in ourselves? That we recognize ourselves equally as culprits and victims? This would put us for the duration of the movie in a state of confused identity, torn between these two options, caught between the fronts and constantly tempted to switch from one side to the other. Our identity would hover like a tightrope walker above a gorge.

Is that the deeper reason for the excitement that this genre offers? It's perfectly possible. It's tempting to be bad. Not least because it's quite strenuous to submit on a permanent basis to the numerous rules, regulations, and prohibitions of a decent life. Does evil also fascinate us because the criminal does something we rather reluctantly forbid ourselves to do: flout all the rules and put ourselves with a cold smile above the law? Although it's also true that by no means all manifestations of evil appeal to us equally. We don't, for example, want to spend ages watching tax evaders engaged in their antisocial activities and we can also do without drunken husbands beating their wives. No, it must be about something much more than this. About huge amounts of money, perhaps. And best of all about a matter of life and death.

Perhaps there's another reason for the popularity of the crime movies: they awaken our rather spiritless, languishing love of good, as often also happens in real life, when we only rediscover our love of a person if this is endangered, if it is at stake, and a look into the abyss brings us to our senses. But would that not mean that from time to time we need the stimulus of evil, of the gruesome and the terrible, in order to put ourselves morally to rights again? Are we therefore dependent on a regular supply of evil visions in order to continue to be good? And if so — does that not indicate how delicate our moral constitution is, and how dependent we are on evil?

After all, at least as far as our conscious will is concerned, we can be certain that we long for order to be restored, we want to see decency, love, and justice winning at the end of all fights and quarrels. Coquetry probably also plays a part in our weakness for evil, we probably aren't serious about it and the final triumph of good is always a release. Our faith in the good order of this world can be shaken, but must not be undermined. In view of the threat represented by evil in the real world, this would be fatal. On the one hand because we have a tendency towards evil. And on the other hand because it damages us irreparably.

Do we have a tendency towards evil?

I fear this is the case, at least that is what experience shows us. We might wish for the victory of good, but we are poorly armed to defend it. While the vices hone themselves, the virtues must be honed by lengthy practice and constantly demonstrated by convincing examples. Evil requires no effort, it suits our fundamental laziness and our preference for effortless solutions, but good requires effort and is always endangered.

If we think of Alipius, the childhood friend of Saint Augustine, it was a huge effort for him to suppress his enthusiasm for gladiator fights when he became a Christian, but it literally took only a moment to cancel out all this hard work. After all, we know how quickly it's possible to get carried away by something that we should deny ourselves if we are sensible: this is an everyday experience that doesn't only occur in front of the baker's shop window. We must be permanently awake, otherwise we let ourselves get away with too much, as the psychologist Alexander Mitscherlich suddenly realized from his own experience. When going through a life crisis he established that every new day required fresh exertion, conscious rebellion against the laziness, negligence, mindlessness, and coldness of everyday life. The Apostle Paul sounds almost desperate when he writes about the same experience in the Letter to the Romans: "For I do not do the good I want, but the evil I do not want is what I do."

It can in case hardly be claimed that good has an easy time of it with us, and it doesn't lead us into temptation either. If we reject a dishonorable offer, we will not be left with the feeling of having succumbed to seduction but will rather have had to force ourselves to resist, possibly after an internal struggle.

But why do we nevertheless make the effort to lead an honest life, in spite of the allure of evil? Only for fear of punishment?

One answer would be because we shrink from evil for good reason. Because we have had experience of it and perhaps even experienced the shattering, elemental impact evil can have on a life. The moment we ourselves become victims, namely, evil loses all its ambivalence and fascination. The seductively smiling mask of temptation is instantly removed and there is the horned visage which we know from the images of the devil in paintings — or the grin of the sadist from the cult movie *Clockwork Orange* by Stanley Kubrick.

It is, once again, uncanny. People don't just get over bad experiences. They are marked by them, maybe even for the rest of their days, and nothing can erase the brand marks from their souls, not even all the positive experiences they have in the course of their lives. One experience is enough — and it doesn't even have to entail massive physical or emotional damage. The betrayal of a friend, the swindling of a business partner, the indifference of a mother may be sufficient to make us suspicious, wary or disheartened forever, and sometimes a spiteful word thoughtlessly dropped into the conversation is all it takes. An encounter with evil can be traumatizing and even if it's a person's only such experience, everything good in the world seems to be powerless against the one injustice that has been suffered.

Of course it doesn't have to be like this. We normally categorize minor disappointments under the heading of "learning from experience" and a person who is unable to do this or is much too trusting is labelled naïve. But for those who have once felt themselves to be the target of cold, calculating or even unintentional, thoughtless malice, a crack opens up in the ground on which they stand. The existence of such an experience deprives them of the basis of trust that carries people through life. And it's virtually impossible to close this crack. If a person's basic trust has been damaged it can at best only be patched up. A remnant of suspicion or uncertainty will remain.

How does this happen?

In this context I am reminded of the story of a family feud, a permanent dispute between siblings — nothing very dramatic and yet enough to spoil the lives of all concerned. It happened in Italy and is soon told.

Three siblings had inherited a country house in Tuscany from their parents. All three were married and their ages ranged from late forties to early fifties. The two brothers had fallen out, always avoided contact with one another and did not want to meet in the country house. Although it was actually necessary for them to talk and make decisions, this was impossible for them and they instead used the third member of the family, the sister, as an intermediary. She took over this task with every intention of contributing to the family peace. However, she soon realized she was being misused for the communication of insults and reproaches as well as instructions from the one brother to the other. One day the brothers would ban each other from entering the house, another day individual family members or the entire family would be banned, or one family would occupy the house shortly before the arrival of the others, so that they were forced to turn back. And now the sister was caught between the fronts and was constantly being accused of siding more with one party than the other, in other words of being a traitor.

The brothers' ingenuity at thinking up new ways to be mean to one another was inexhaustible. The feud had taken on a life of its own and was only marginally about the use of the inherited country house. The two men made life difficult for each other and together made it difficult for the sister, who was still trying to please everybody, only to receive fresh reproaches from both sides. But the most amazing thing about it was not only that this method gave no one an obvious advantage — but that with time the sister also despaired and the adults of the feuding families became depressed, and still nobody wanted to give in. "What am I doing wrong?" the sister once asked me, when she was forced to admit the failure of her intermediary efforts. "Nothing," I replied. "Under these circumstances it's not possible to do anything right. This kind of wickedness is totally unpredictable. The only principle it follows is doing the greatest possible damage."

Crazy, you would think. Insane. But that's exactly the point. This is where the explanation for the frighteningly permanent effect of evil must lie. It hits us unexpectedly. Every move, every maneuver is unpredictable. It doesn't follow any logic, or only the logic of maliciousness. The only reliable thing about evil is its arbitrariness. This is why it leaves us helpless. This is why it shatters our trust in existence as a whole. This is why we suddenly no longer understand the world.

The Hamburg sociologist Jan Philipp Reemtsma calls it "the logic of terror." Writing of the Nazi concentration camps, he says that every attempt of the prisoners to get a picture of what was happening was doomed to failure. The concentration camp staff never did what they expected. Nor did it help to imagine the worst — at any time something else could happen. It was therefore impossible to adjust to the grueling circumstances. The logic of terror is unpredictable. It shatters, demoralizes, makes us lose our minds ... This seems to me to describe evil in its broadest sense. It is preposterous. It often cannot be associated with the person from whom it emanates, in other words, it just wouldn't have been expected from this particular individual. Just as the sister of the two brothers in my example would never have believed they would both go as far with their war of attrition as to destroy their own peace of mind.

They preferred to lose all joy in life rather than stop retaliating ... The only reason I can see for such behavior is to retain a pathetic feeling of superiority for all time by preventing what is seen as a defeat. Maybe satisfaction also plays a role, satisfaction that the thirst for revenge has been quenched or "justice" done. The price of such minimal benefits is exorbitant and is having to be paid in our example by three families, but we repeatedly have to ask ourselves what bad people get from their wickedness? To what extent is it worth it to them?

What we have studied so far in this chapter is the objective side of evil. The side that is perceived by everyone — the ugly, destructive side. By everyone, it must be said, who experiences evil as a victim or an observer. But what about the perpetrators of evil? I will call them here perpetrators without using the word in a criminal sense. How do they see evil? What is their goal? Are they acting with the intention of causing harm, spreading terror or hurting?

Our spontaneous response is to say of course they are. What characterizes perpetrators is obviously their malice, the urge to hurt, harm, humiliate or do mischief to a greater or lesser degree. The killer wants to kill, the swindler wants to swindle, the insulter wants to insult, and it's all about harming and hurting another person. But is this true?

Let's go back to the example of the boy with the spider. "It was fun," he said. Well, the fact that his sister had reacted in panic shows that he really hadn't been nice, he must have been aware of that, and had anyone else terrified her he would probably have intervened. Nevertheless, he was tempted to be nasty in this small way. Why? Probably because as a perpetrator he could look forward to an experience of a very special kind: the brief rush of satisfaction in gaining power over his sister by means of the spider. After all, it worked. At the moment of his prank he was vastly superior to his helpless and defenseless sister. It was entirely at his discretion to stop the nasty game or to drive his sister even further to despair. She was at his mercy and what gave her the greatest pain gave him a brief but most pleasant feeling of omnipotence. The ugly deed had therefore paid off for him. It had, as he said, been fun.

As you can see, the concept of malevolence can't be trusted absolutely. At least evil doesn't seem to be the main intention of the perpetrator. An evil deed is committed rather in order to achieve something that the perpetrator finds pleasing, good and right — in this case the feeling of unlimited superiority. We therefore have to assume that with every insult, intrigue, and betrayal, evildoers are trying to improve their position with respect to another person. This probably applies even to the absurd dispute about the country house. Even here something must have been at stake that the hostile parties saw as their most precious possession, to be protected at all costs. Perhaps it was their pride or their singularly correct view of things — something at any rate that it was worth making each other's lives hell for. As absurd it sounds, it can't be put in any other way: basically all bad persons want something good. They ultimately always want the best. Namely the best for them. Scholastic theologians in the Middle Ages put it like this: Evil cannot be an end in itself. It cannot be desired at all. Evil is only the means to an end from which the perpetrator hopes to gain an advantage, a benefit, a pleasure or liberty. In other words: for the bad person evil is usually a pleasure.

Perpetrators are possibly right in denying any evil intention.

However, what do they know about themselves at all, about their own motives, their own reasons? How accountable are people to whom evil presents a face that is completely different from the one it presents to their victims. People who can justify their actions to themselves as evidence of personal initiative, ingenuity or superiority or as an act of self defense, compensatory justice or simply as fun. People to whom, in short, evil seems good, in other words advantageous.

My fear that it might not be possible to grasp evil seems at this point to be coming true. This is truly uncanny. For what can be more perplexing than two people who at the moment of encounter do not seem to be inhabiting the same universe? Here on the one hand is the victim to whom evil only brings horror because what happens does not fit into his or her world. And there on the other is the perpetrator who steps out of the sphere of a binding global order by shamelessly doing evil in the spirit of the innocent fortune seeker. Can there be a greater contradiction between two people?

An insurmountable abyss opens up between the victim and the perpetrator. Every connection is broken off. This abyss is not so frightening in the context of normal everyday meanness, but it's there and always opens up, either briefly or for a lifetime when evil asserts itself. What is annoying or terrible for one person is quite possibly a pleasure, a stimulating drug for another person. There is no consciousness of guilt that can prevent the deed. The intentions are good and the attendant circumstances are taken into account. These are the two faces of evil: threat and temptation.

None of this, on the other hand, applies to good.

Good remains the same, from whatever perspective. It never changes, just like the painters' depictions of God. It spells reassurance, consolation, and gladness for everyone involved. It is thus unspectacular. Hence its low degree of fascination, its minimal potential to excite. It's not an invigorating drug like evil — at least it doesn't have such an instant effect. It doesn't immediately make our blood boil. It's undramatic. According to our understanding of the world it's simply what is normal, wisest and most reasonable. So does this confirm that evil is the result of compulsiveness and instability? And is good always to be understood as the result of sensible self-control?

This is what we must examine next.

4

Reason versus emotion

Who or what is to blame for evil? Mankind has always searched for an answer to this question and the diagnoses are as variable and numerous as the cures and remedies that have been prescribed for evil in the course of time. In the following chapters I shall bring together answers from 3,000 years of history; but first I will try to clarify for myself the role of reason and the emotions in this context. Are drives and emotions really the gateway for evil? Is our moral control center governed by reason? Or is it more complicated than this?

It might help to start with a little moral experiment. Imagine it's Sunday morning and you're on your way to church. You already have some money ready because the homeless man will be standing in front of the door holding his hand out. You know him, he's there every Sunday; it's basically his regular place, and you always hand over a few coins. Then you stop when you get a bit closer because it irritates you to see that today there are two people. On the right-hand side of the entrance is the homeless man you know and on the left-hand side is a stranger with a white plastic cup in his hand, who is evidently from South - Eastern Europe. And suddenly you realize you have a problem.

A moral problem. For how you should behave now? Give something to the homeless man and not to the stranger? Or give them both something? Or neither of them anything? The fact is that the homeless in your city have divided the various locations between them and it is an unwritten law that no one can try and take another's lucrative regular spot in front of a church. What the strange beggar is doing from the perspective of the homeless man is a breach of good manners and basically an impertinence. He's invading his territory and reducing his takings. This shouldn't be supported, and you don't want to support it either. So do you only give the homeless man something and ignore the beggar?

Actually, you think, you should see off the beggar. No, you contradict yourself immediately, there would be no legal basis for that and you might have to use force, which wouldn't only be inappropriate, it would also create an ugly scene: look at that, people would say, the weary and heavy laden are not tolerated in front of the church, of all places . . . The situation can't be changed anyway. So do you act like Solomon and give something to both of them?

Absolutely not, you protest. Then the strange beggar's brazenness would even be rewarded. And how would the homeless man see my behavior? Mightn't this give him the impression that I deny his claim on this location? Then the solution can only be to give the homeless person something as usual, and the foreign beggar nothing.

On the other hand . . .

Wouldn't that be shabby? This beggar is a human being too. He too has feelings, and is not begging for fun. He might possibly be poorer than the homeless man. A demonstrative rejection would in any case hurt him personally and he would feel like an outcast. Doesn't the one deserve the same compassion as the other? Wouldn't it be more human to treat both equally? This means giving something to both of them. But if you still want to give the intruder nothing as a punishment, all that remains is to give nothing to either of them.

However, that would be even shabbier, you say to yourself. Then I would be punishing the homeless man, who is already being punished enough by the unwelcome competition. First the stranger is making his life difficult and now I am as well. It must not come to this. In short, everything in you rebels against giving the one in the right the same treatment as the one in the wrong. So nevertheless give the homeless man something and ignore the beggar? In the meantime you've got to the church door. There's no more time for deliberation, now you have to act. And what now carries more weight for you? The demand for strictly equal treatment? The commitment to general compassion, regardless of the person? Or the dictates of decency, fairness, and rightfulness? So give nothing to either? Give something to both? Or only make your usual contribution to the homeless man?

I am afraid there's no really satisfactory solution to this. However, it's not the outcome I'm interested in. What I want to prove is that for moral problems there are no standard solutions. Nor can they be solved instinctively. Each problem must be thought through and it is quite amazing how much has to be taken into account even in a minor case like this. There are arguments and counter-arguments to be weighed up, and our reason comes into play — so in fact we are obliged to say that if we take moral problems seriously we are called on to exercise our reason. It's not the emotions that call the shots.

Nevertheless, we don't try to resolve our moral dilemma on the basis of practical usefulness or theoretical correctness. The basis of our deliberations is the values that form the framework for our behavior and the key question is what should our decision be if we want to give as much pleasure as possible or, if this is not an option, if we want to limit the inevitable disappointment as much as possible? And now it gets complicated. For political issues one can use political arguments, for economic issues economic arguments, but when making moral decisions the arguments are taken from several very different areas, as has already been seen. Law and a sense of justice play a role, religious and philosophical considerations must be taken into account, the social reality plays a part, and even sport contributes a crucial standard, namely fairness.

And because in moral matters it's not only about the other person but also about ourselves, we must include the economic sphere too as a marginal consideration: what amount are we willing to give? How much is the other person's happiness worth to us?

As you can see, the application of moral principles requires considerable reflection. We have to be clear about the scope of our moral decision-making, we have to make a clear separation between different interests and weigh them against each other, we have to take the numerous aspects of a case into account — and all this is done by reasoning. Emotions are not much use to us here. We can give money to the more appealing person or for the sake of simplicity give something to both or nothing to either, but this would not be morally justifiable behavior and in a more serious case it would be irresponsible.

There is much more at stake in the following case. It is the most famous example of a conflict between reason and instincts, namely the temptation of Jesus in the desert. In Matthew's Gospel it is related as follows:

> When he was baptized, Jesus withdrew into the rocky wilderness of the Judean desert and stayed there for 40 days in complete solitude, fasting, and deep in prayer. When he was overpowered by hunger, the tempter came to him: "If you are the Son of God," he said, "command these stones to become loaves of bread." "One word from you would be enough." Jesus answered: "It is written: 'One does not live by bread alone, but by every word that comes from the mouth of God.'" Then the devil took him to the holy city and placed him on the pinnacle of the temple, saying to him, "If you are the Son of God, throw yourself down;" for what can happen to you? "It is written: 'He will command his angels concerning you', and 'On their hands they will bear you up, so that you will not dash your foot against a stone.'" Jesus said to him: "Again it is written, 'Do not put the Lord your God to the test.'" Then, the devil took him to a very high mountain and showed him all the kingdoms of the world and their splendor;

and he said to him, "All these I will give you, if you will fall down and worship me." Jesus said to him, "Away with you, Satan! for it is written, 'Worship the Lord your God, and serve only him.'" Then the devil left him. . . .

An amazing story: The devil argues. He could also have simply offered the starving Jesus a piece of bread, thereby asking him to eat out of his hand like a dog. But evil is not so coarse. Satan argues. He tries with logic. We become witnesses of a scholarly dispute, arguments are exchanged and finally the tempter admits defeat. Why is Jesus the winner here? Because he exposes the illusory rationality of the satanic arguments. What sounds reasonable and plausible is in reality absurd. It is supposed to lead Jesus astray. That is the temptation.

It's all a complicated game. Satan seems to pay homage to Jesus as the Son of God, but takes general human weaknesses as his starting point, the classical human weaknesses, so to speak, like the survival instinct and the craving for recognition. Are you hungry? What are you waiting for — abuse your divine power to satisfy your needs. You trust the promises of God? What are you waiting for? Put him to the test right here, abuse his promises with a frivolous experiment! You're striving for the greatest conceivable power? What are you waiting for? Worship me, nothing is impossible. This is familiar to us. People can always be tempted to satisfy personal needs, seize power, and at the same time make fun of God and so it can also be tried with God's son. Only he would no longer be the Son of God afterwards. He wouldn't even be a man. At least not the one he wants to be.

And Jesus resists. With arguments that expose the real intentions of the satanic arguments. They are self-destructive offers in the guise of reason. What sounds like liberation and wish-fulfillment would make him dependent. Jesus however shows what it is most sensible to do, namely prevent oneself and one's soul from harm. You can see that this temptation story touches on the problem of identity — who do I want to be? What is compatible with my own image of myself and what is not? There are shades here of the well-known motif of the man who sells his soul to the devil. I will not elaborate on this here, as the topic will occupy us later on.

In summary it can be said that evil follows the logic of making the destructive or self-destructive plausible. And good uses reason and exposes the logic of evil as illusory rationality. An important distinction, but one it is often difficult to make in real life because evil primarily appears in the guise of what is obvious and appropriate, what is reasonable. It still doesn't mean anything if something sounds as if it makes sense. How often has reason justified the most horrific atrocities, and to this very day unbelievable crimes are perpetrated by rationally thinking and coolly calculating people. This can be illustrated by a report in the newspaper *Frankfurter Allgemeine Zeitung* in March 2014 about what has been happening on the peninsula of Sinai. It told an incredible story:

> Unnoticed by the outside world, refugees from Eritrea have been tortured and murdered in Sinai for many years. It's a business. Traffickers kidnap the refugees forcibly from their camps in Sudan, bring them in trucks over the Egyptian border and sell them to Bedouins in Sinai. These people in turn torture them until they divulge the addresses of their relatives in their country of origin. Their sufferings do not end there, because they continue to be tortured to encourage their families to pay up. When the ransom does finally arrive, the victims have often reached the limits of what they can endure and all they are good for is being cut open to remove their organs. Ransom and organ trafficking is the business model and everyone makes money, the traffickers, the border officials, and the Bedouin clans.

Even that is somehow based on reason — making money from people by recycling them. The mafia operate on a similarly rational basis, the concentration camps were rationally planned and managed, and we finally justify ourselves with reason and expediency when we want to put a gloss on something we've done that's not very nice. There are always good reasons; you only have to make evil look halfway reasonable and it passes freely through all rational controls. A lack of sober reflection and considered action cannot at any rate be established in the above case, but evil still triumphs. And if you look at our criminal code you'll see that calculation and rational action can even be crucial for establishing the degree of guilt.

One of the criteria forensic psychologists use to assess the criminal responsibility of perpetrators is the "planning degree" of the deed. The psychologist Claudia Brockmann explains why this is also used to measure guilt. She writes: "The more intensively a deed was prepared, the more strongly the behavioral pattern on which it was based is rooted in the personality of the offenders. It apparently didn't suddenly come over them, but the risks and the things that fascinated them had long been played out in their minds. They therefore had more opportunity to consider the injustice of their deeds, to imagine the suffering of their victims, and to ask themselves the question: "Do I really want this?" In other words, the more deliberately offenders proceed, the more reprehensible are their crimes. Apparently you can get just as carried away while thinking clearly as you can when the emotions get the upper hand.

Apparently we can't therefore solely rely on fully functioning powers of reasoning when deciding for or against evil. They offer us no guarantee. There must be something more.

What is the most horrifying aspect in the case of the tortured Eritreans? I would say that it is the total lack of compassion we see here. Apparently the ability to feel compassion is only rudimentary in the perpetrators or is very selective. The previously mentioned abyss that opens up between offender and victim could not in any case be deeper — the screams of pain of the latter don't reach the ears of the former. Conscience might of course differ according to culture, but in our perception of humanity, compassion is a necessary precondition of good and I will therefore stick to my Christian standards: anyone who does not respond to the sufferings of others is at least pandering to evil and conversely nothing good can happen in this world that does not flow from an all-embracing compassion. Even the internal debate occasioned by the two men begging at the church door would be pointless without compassion; it wouldn't even arise because we could then make things easy for ourselves and wouldn't even have to notice them. But shouldn't we take this farther? Don't all great gestures of humanity come straight from the heart?

Here I think particularly of the father in the parable of the prodigal son as told in Luke's Gospel: the second son, the black sheep of the family, returns home dejected and remorseful after years of a dissolute life. He has squandered his inheritance, fears his father's anger, and is prepared to serve him as a slave. When his father sees him coming, he runs to meet him and embraces him with a cry of joy. And if this were not enough, he has a calf slaughtered for him and organizes a lavish reunion feast. What an outbreak of paternal love! He does not consider the pros and cons for long, he unthinkingly obeys the dictates of his heart and allows himself to be overwhelmed by his feelings. Of course, the issues here are not good and evil, not even right and wrong, only severity or mildness, punishment or forgiveness. Nevertheless — it is wonderful and liberating how this father overcomes many years of trouble in one moment and allows himself to be carried away by his deepest feelings. Reason would have told him to call his son to account first.

And if we look at the God of the Bible himself . . . Actually he bears little resemblance to the serene old man looking down on us from church walls and old paintings. He's by no means imperturbable. This God suffers, gets angry, is jealous, loves, gets excited, also sends a flood and says of himself, I will spew out the lukewarm. Those who are neither cold nor hot. The hesitant, the half-hearted, the reasoners. Apparently this God is himself a passionate being and one can hardly imagine God differently, because passion is energy and the motor of all change, development, and renewal.

Thank goodness there is this enormous emotional driving force. And, given the seductive power of evil, mustn't we rise above ourselves? But the passionless person crumbles. This is why Hegel says that nothing great in the world has been accomplished without passion. A morality that condemns passion wholesale is a dead and hypocritical morality. . . And what about love? The burning passion of those in love? Here reason in any case has no place and even charity without feeling a certain amount of warmth towards one's neighbor would smack of simply doing one's duty. But shouldn't we then abandon the explanation of evil as the result of our irrational impulses? Shouldn't we at least equally mistrust reason?

However . . . now I am having some doubts. Isn't burning passion rather too similar to being drunk with power? Don't both of these mean losing control of oneself and at the same time gaining power over another person or many people? Isn't this a condition in which a person can no longer differentiate between good and evil? Aren't bankers who irresponsibly juggle with billions, rip off their customers or are rewarded for disastrous transactions with a bonus in millions on a par with lovers? Can we rely on any feeling at all, if evil not only produces abhorrence, but also pleasure?

Looked at in the cold light of day, our susceptibility for the irrational is possibly no less uncanny than evil, and finally it might well be concluded that extreme caution is advised. That it would be better if the wings of people's passion were clipped to prevent the worst.

5

The gods are to blame?

Who or what is to blame for evil?

Perhaps the answer is best sought by going back through the centuries, beginning with the ancient Greeks and Israelites. The Greek myths, the Bible, philosophy, and theology are treasure troves of answers to our question. At any rate, there are 28 centuries to discuss and when you open the Odyssey — the earliest document I would like to consult — you find right at the beginning an irreconcilable difference of opinion between gods and humans as to who or what is to blame?

It is a tremendous scene. Homer has the gods meet in the residence of Zeus on Mount Olympus. Athene can hardly wait to speak in support of her favorite, Odysseus, but first Zeus has to give a keynote speech and give vent to his disappointment in the human race. "What do the mortals accuse the gods of?" he exclaims. "All evil comes from us alone, they cry; and nevertheless the fools create their own misery, which runs counter to their destiny." Then he gives as an example for the shortsightedness of human beings the bloody deed of Aegisthus, who has killed Agamemnon against all the warnings of the gods. He has thus dug his own grave, says Zeus, because Agamemnon's son Orestes will revenge his father. But, reading between the lines, what he's really saying is "That's typical. That's what mortals are like, defiant and obtuse like children and — to put it bluntly — intellectually somewhat limited. Rather than think in advance of the consequences, they would rather wallow in self-pity afterwards and complain that "I couldn't help myself, the gods are to blame, they have imposed this terrible fate on me . . ."

With this Zeus hits the nail on the head. This is just what the people are saying. They would never think of ascribing the ceaseless feuds, fights, and slaughter to themselves and to what the gods see as their boundless stupidity. Instead, the Greeks of early antiquity see themselves as the gods' whipping boys. They believe in their innocence even though to our way of thinking everything argues against it. Yet they do recognize objective guilt. There is evil, yes, it occurs constantly, but the cause lies with the gods. As they understand it, you can both be guilty and remain innocent and as a perpetrator simultaneously be a victim, namely the victim of a ruthless fate, in other words the victim of the gods. In the ancient drama, Clytemnestra is not horrified at herself after she has murdered her husband, but instead accuses those particular demons who arouse the blood lust in human beings. And the chorus on the stage comments on the terrible deed with the horrified proclamation that "There is nothing that happens on earth that is not the work of the gods!"

Everything is of course their work. But this applies especially to evil. Because it is irrational and against all reason, because it comes over one like the frenzy that overcomes the warrior in battle and therefore cannot possible originate in a rational being. It must arise from a mysterious world, it can be attributed only to the inexplicable whims of the gods. Guilty? Maybe. But not responsible.

An easy way out, you might say. But it is everything but easy. It is as uncanny as evil. It is the honest confession of capitulation before the incomprehensible and an expression of a remorseful, helpless realism — life means being at the mercy of the gods, life means being guilty and basically what the Greek myths are is a price list: this is what life costs, and this is the price you have to pay for it, and you are not asked, but the sum is automatically deducted from your life. From your first cry as a newborn you are burdened by a mortgage you have to repay by savoring the imposed suffering and knowingly-unknowingly making mistakes that will rebound on you. This can't reassure you and it certainly can't comfort you.

For the ancient Greeks, evil takes possession of man via passion. And this comes from outside. It is something impersonal. Even now we still have an inner laboratory that produces horrors we want nothing to do with, but for the people of antiquity passion is a kind of madness, which comes out of nowhere and looks for a victim. When attacked by it they enter a state that appears inexplicable as soon as the passion subsides. Which does not make the situation any better, as I've already said, because no psychologist or priest can take away susceptibility to the irrational. Evil in the ancient world can't be reduced to a remediable, mental defect, it remains an objective, harrowing but ultimately mysterious fact.

If we now turn our attention to Israel, it first presents a similar picture. To describe the unflinching sinfulness of his compatriots, in around 600 BC the Prophet Jeremiah resorts to a dramatic comparison: he sees the same animalistic sexual urges at work with them as with rutting camels or wild asses on heat. And irresponsibility is equally familiar to him. He writes, addressing the people as a whole: "Also on your skirts is found the lifeblood of the innocent poor, though you did not catch them breaking in. Yet in spite of all these things you say, 'I am innocent'. . ." And there's also a revealing text in the Old Testament regarding the relationship of passion and reason, namely in Genesis, the first book of the Bible. The following highly interesting incident is reported from the early days of the people of Israel.

Dina, the daughter of the patriarch Jacob, is seduced by the tribal leader of the city of Shechem and at least mild violence is apparently involved. Nevertheless, on this occasion the ruler of Shechem takes so much pleasure in her that he wants to marry her. He approaches Jacob's sons Simon and Levi asks for their sister's hand, pointing out the economic benefits of this connection, and the sons accept under the condition that all the male inhabitants of Shechem are circumcized. No sooner said than done. But on the third day when the wounds of the circumcized are particularly painful, Simon and Levi and their followers attack Shechem, work themselves into a murderous frenzy and put all the men to the sword — incapacitated as they are. A massacre.

Aside from the treachery, we would speak in this case of particularly serious guilt because of the high degree of planning. And how does father Jacob react, when he learns about the slaughter? He's extremely restrained. In any case, there's no word of reproach. Morally this bloodbath is apparently unobjectionable. If he still can't endorse the actions of his sons, this is because he fears the revenge of the neighboring cities — what if the others band together against him and his family? That is only to be expected! His sons wave away this argument "Should our sister be treated like a whore?" they say tersely. No, it was the proper thing to do and that is the end of that.

The interesting point for me is that the Jewish writer has the same basic approach to the story as a Greek would have had in his day. There's is no question of personal guilt, revenge as a motive is perfectly sufficient, and if once initiated it turns into a murderous frenzy, is this surprising? Where the passions prevail, moderation doesn't stand a chance. And then Jacob has the same basic complaint to make of his sons as Zeus does of the whole human race, namely that they acted without thinking. That they didn't have the wit to foresee the consequences of their actions.

Because in one respect evil is predictable. Once unleashed it can't be reined in again. It always attracts further mischief, it sets off a chain reaction of retaliation. This is the curse of the evil deed: Evil constantly begets evil.

In this ancient world, we encounter an amazing and alienating fact: the enormous emotional resistance, the outrage, the disgust, everything we muster today against evil is scarcely to be found, especially in the Greek world. The Greeks' relationship to evil is much more practical and pragmatic — it does not pay, it rebounds on its originator — and the evildoer is reprimanded for rashness rather than wickedness. Offenders may in turn cite a circumstance that protects them from being reproached for intellectual naivety and thus save face. Since passion is still accepted as a cause and trigger of crime, and as an external force of mysterious origin, passion is perfectly compatible with the self-image of a rational being.

So everyone is served by this — the gods can point to the mortals (and at most send a flood) and the mortals to the gods. There's only one catch: if this is the reasoning, nothing will change. When the buck is constantly passed between the parties the discussion goes round in circles and, strictly speaking, the answer to our initial question "Who or what is to blame for evil?" must be that nobody is to blame.

However, this is not a satisfying result. Especially not in a world in which more and more people in the growing cities are living closer and closer together and have to more or less get along with one another. A minimum sense of responsibility is essential in these circumstances. In the middle of the first millennium, something new thus begins to emerge in Greece and Israel: human beings gradually become responsible and for the first time accountable. Although the two peoples arrive at this by different routes. If people can't combat evil on their own, civilization's got to help, say the Greeks. If people don't succeed on their own, only God can help, say the Jews.

Rational persons should be upgraded to become moral persons and turned into reliable, trustworthy companions. To achieve this, they must be tamed or, as the Roman poet Lucretius puts it, their wildness must be broken. How? First by supervision, because control by others comes before self control.

In Greece this is done by the Polis, the society of the urban community. In order to ease the situation for everyone, pressure has to be put on individuals, and over time people acquire as citizens the ability to put pressure on themselves. In the crowdedness of the cities, the good of others is a more pressing factor, and this means being considerate, controlling oneself, taking responsibility for one's behavior, and taking the consequences. Gradually people become accustomed to searching for evil in themselves, in their own imperfection. They discover with increasing penetration that it's something to do with them and that at the end, in a state of excellence, it might even be possible to deal with evil through their own efforts.

This is what is being heatedly debated. In 5th-century Athens, people ask earnestly what concrete measures can be taken against evil. Socrates, for example, looks at the now acute ethical questions from all angles in detailed dialogs. How can one become a better person? Can individual virtues be freely acquired (to some extent through coaching), or do you have to train your character as a whole? How can the irrational be restrained as far as is possible? The dark and uncanny should now also be made accessible to reason, by talking about and investigating it and in this way taking the sting out of it. How harmless and reasonable the talk about evil suddenly sounds can be illustrated by a short example from the *Protagoras,* one of the Socratic dialogs written by Plato. It says:

> Because nobody is voluntarily a bad person, but a bad person is so because of the bad nature of his body and an upbringing without guidance . . . It is more the fault of the begetter than of the begotten person, more the fault of the educator than of the person being educated and certainly one must endeavor through education, employment, and knowledge to escape the bad and take possession of its opposite.

So here we have the method of civilization: observe each other, exert influence on each other, and make a joint effort to strengthen the defenses against evil. Wild and uncontrolled behavior stems from evil, but under the stern gaze of prudent teachers it should be possible to tame the irrational impulses successfully. It's only hinted at once in this quote that nature has some say too and the body as the seat of arbitrary urges could foil you.

All in all, developments in Greece suddenly sound very reassuring. It's as if evil was already halfway under control. Philosophy is the main source of hope at this time and its message is, it's not the gods who are to blame, not fate, and not even the fatal tendency of mankind to lose its head. What is to blame is the unformed natural condition of mankind in the past. But this can be overcome. With the progress of civilization, human beings will also change for the better. Basically they are made for good with their brilliant mental powers — they just still have to continue working on themselves.

Incidentally, 2000 years later the unformed natural condition will be called self-imposed immaturity and its conquest called enlightenment. And the same hopes will be pinned on it . . .

Such optimism doesn't exist in Israel. Here good and evil play out in a different dimension. What the Greece call wickedness, the Jews call sin and is a much more significant concept — "the inclination of the human heart is evil from youth" as God declares after the flood. This is basically true and in principle nothing can be changed. After all there are means of purification.

However the benchmark for the Jews is extremely high. The God of the Jews is much more demanding than the Greek gods. He doesn't merely vent his displeasure about the people as Zeus does in a short speech and otherwise pursue his own interests. He says, "I am holy and you too should be holy," in other words, he expects his people to be like him. This can't be achieved by one's own efforts, this is not a reasonable expectation. This is an extremely stringent demand that presupposes a profound spiritual renewal of the person, a real inner transformation that in turn is possible only with the help of God. The poet of Psalm 51 thus turns to God and says, "Create in me a clean heart, O God, and put a new and right spirit within me."

However, the desired purity of heart also demands the utmost effort from the individual. It affects everything, the person's

thoughts, behavior, and whole way of life, and the goal of the pure
heart is only achieved when everything is done according to the
will of God as understood from the written commandments and the
prophets. Those who want to get this far must undergo incessant
self-examination. They must in fact know, as only God can know,
precisely what their motives are, and basically see themselves
through the eyes of God. For nothing escapes God. He scrutinizes
us. "You know when I sit down and when I rise up; you discern my
thoughts from far away. You search out my path and my lying down,
and are acquainted with all my ways," as it says in Psalm 139. This
leads the Psalm writer on to say "Search me, O God, and know my
heart; test me and know my thoughts."

Doesn't that sound familiar? Isn't God being assigned the role
of psychoanalyst? Seen in this light you feel as if you are witnessing
the birth of psychoanalysis, more than 2000 years before Sigmund
Freud. And just as psychoanalysis gave an entire society the idea of
concerning themselves with their own inner life, so this omniscient,
omnipresent God instructs the people of that time to illuminate
every corner of their inner selves. With the aim of becoming like
God, pure and ultimately holy.

Become holy like God? Isn't that completely unrealistic?
Isn't that inflated self-esteem? This utopian ardor is even more
disconcerting in the 21st century, as through experience we've
become very humble with respect to our moral capabilities. But
mankind was not always so modest and the Jewish project of a pure
heart doesn't seem any more audacious to me than the attempt
of the Greeks to achieve excellence. At any rate, both visions of
perfection are based on a courageous optimism, and only the way
the people try to achieve this differs. To break the uncanny power
of evil, the Greeks submit themselves to the rule of reason in the
hope of gaining complete self-control. The Jews rely on their God
to achieve the same thing and imitate him in the hope of being able
to identify evil right from the outset and eliminate it. In Greece, the
virtue of the enlightened citizen is to gradually oust evil from the

community; in Israel the attack on evil is targeted, since it is to be tracked down in one's own heart and nipped in the bud before it can spread and invade the whole person. Or to put it in a nutshell: the Greeks try it with community rule and the Jews with self-rule.

In ancient Israel, one thing is still absent: the notion of personal liability for one's own deeds, individual responsibility. The idea that an individual can be guilty is widespread, but guilt is transferable. To one's descendants, for example. Ezekiel, a 6th-century BC prophet, cites a common Jewish proverb which says "The parents have eaten sour grapes, and the children's teeth are set on edge." Guilt can thus be passed down from the parents to the children. As a result, the children have to atone for the sins of their fathers (or mothers) and the latter can hope to be exempted. What this means is simply that with a bit of luck the consequences of an evil deed will only be felt in the next generation.

And now Ezekiel appears and says no, everyone only has to pay for what he or she has done wrong, because people are responsible for themselves alone. "A child shall not suffer for the iniquity of a parent, nor a parent suffer for the iniquity of a child." This is incredible but that's what the message is. This is how God speaks through the mouth of the prophet. His audience finds this hard to believe. They are unwilling to relinquish the idea that guilt can be redistributed or shifted in case of need. They would prefer to think God could be wrong about this; the idea of perhaps getting away with things is too tempting. Ultimately, however, men like Ezekiel initiate the same process in Israel as the flourishing of civilization in the cities of Greece: human beings gradually learn to see themselves as accountable, self-responsible people.

The time when one can cite the gods, fate or ancestors as an excuse thus comes to an end. From now on, people are expected to look for evil within themselves — and credited with being able to take responsibility.

6

The contours of evil

The previous chapter gave us an overview of the first millennium BC. I could continue my survey of history and will certainly do so, because we are missing two millennia. For the moment, however, I would like to pause in this account. This is because it has become clear to me that the ancient Greeks and Jews differ not only in their strategy of combating evil, but also in their assessment of the essence of evil. And since we have still not really clarified this point, I would like to examine it now.

For the Greeks, I have the impression that evil is something akin to a breakdown. As if man, to put it in modern terms, were comparable to a technical installation, which normally works as planned, but because of its complexity is susceptible to failure — breakdowns that can extend to the collapse of the whole system cannot be excluded with absolute certainty. Evil in this case is like a sort of industrial accident that can be rectified with the right methods, and one day can perhaps be excluded altogether. The interesting thing about this is that a very similar view has gained sway with us in recent decades. Even modern Western society is convinced that evil is based on a number of factors that only need to be corrected — at any rate it's not so deep-seated that it can't be dealt with by means of education, training, and therapy. For the Jews, on the other hand, evil is as it were built into the design of the human race right from the beginning, and the world is therefore inconceivable without evil. This view is more pessimistic but probably more realistic — the fact that there is no remedy against it, that evil has accompanied mankind persistently throughout the centuries and proved resistant to all social, political, and cultural developments seems to me to support the second concept.

But let's look at this again more closely. Perhaps the following questions can be clarified on the basis of examples and observations.

Where does evil start? At what point does our behavior stop being harmless? How far can you go, from what moment on have you gone too far and why can you (at least after the fact) say with certainty that you have stepped over the line between good and evil?

The best approach seems to me to leave aside the unambiguous cases and look at the borderline cases of evil. Those cases where one has the feeling that something evil has happened without being able to pinpoint it. I will therefore choose my examples from a moral grey area, where evil is in a sense at an early stage or only suspected and hard to prove. When does responsible behavior turn into irresponsible behavior? Where exactly do you draw the line?

Example 1. In Manhattan a man is hit and crushed by a subway train. He's pushed by the crowd onto the tracks, tries to get back onto the platform but doesn't succeed, because the edge of the platform is too high. A few seconds before the train hits him, someone takes a photo of him. It shows the man trying to pull himself up and a platform full of people. None of them moved, nobody helped him . . .

It's picture that fills you with despair. Something has to happen, everyone can see a life is at stake, but nothing happens. Do they all say to themselves, "It's not my fault?" Do the people standing there even look for an excuse for themselves? That would imply that they at least feel they are being addressed. Who knows, perhaps they even feel sorry for the man. But this doesn't lead to anything. One person takes a picture instead of helping the man out of this fatal trap.

What happened there? We sense that this was no ordinary

accident. After thinking about it for longer we also feel something outrageous happened. But there's no offender. No one was responsible. No one was guilty. The guilt evaporates in the crowd of the subway station and with this the crime is solved. But can't we smell, taste, and feel the presence of evil here? Doesn't a toxic cloud hang over this apathetic, indifferent crowd? However perplexed we are, the incident still smacks of irresponsibility.

Example 2. This is taken from everyday school life. During the break a boy drops the wrapping from his chocolate bar on the ground in the school yard. A young teacher standing next to him asks him to pick it up. He grins at her and says, "Wasn't me." "But I saw you," she replies. "So what," he retorts, "have you got proof?" Then he leaves the teacher standing and walks off . . .

It's not as bad as all that, you might say. The damage is not worth mentioning: a piece of waste paper on the ground and an angry teacher. Must this be labelled evil? Isn't it much too harmless for that?

Nevertheless, you wince. Since there is much more to it than insolence. This time the irresponsibility is tangible.

Here is a person immune to rebuke, an unscrupulous person playing a sophisticated power game, and for a moment we are the witnesses of a humiliation. In addition, the teacher will probably capitulate, will sooner or later look away in the schoolyard as her colleagues already do. So the damage is by no means minor and this is a manifestation of evil — but where did it start? Difficult to say. The boy's sense of guilt must in any case already have been eroded.

What do the first two example show us? It looks as if there is certainly a relationship between irresponsibility and evil, but this can be very vague. The one can't be completely equated with the other, and evil certainly can't be reduced to irresponsibility. In spite of their similarity, the two terms belong nonetheless to two different, if closely related categories.

It's also hard to determine where evil begins. Sometimes it

seems to have long become a habit, as in the second example, sometimes it's only vaguely recognizable, as in the first example, so no line can be drawn to separate it from good. Maybe we'll get a bit further with this if we replace irresponsibility by lack of compassion. Here are two more examples:

Example 3. During the French Revolution, Sanson was the executioner of Paris. A reliable person. He fetched the condemned with his cart from the prison, accompanied them to the guillotine and performed his task with the greatest of skill: beheading the unfortunates so rapidly and smoothly that they were spared all unnecessary suffering. Sanson also didn't participate in the abuse that the public heaped on the victims; on the way to the guillotine he even had a word of comfort for particularly distressed people. Not only a reliable man — a person with a heart . . .

Did evil play a role here at all? Absolutely, from our present perspective: tens of thousands were condemned during the Revolution in summary proceedings, many because of a dismissive remark or a lack of revolutionary zeal, people we would consider innocent. And this man strapped dozens of people to the bench of the guillotine every day, put the iron collar around their necks and dropped the blade. Just the thought of it makes us shudder. What happened in those days in Paris was sheer terror, it was evil in just about its worst form, and Sanson played a leading role in this bloody drama. But he was not lacking in compassion. The abusive taunting of the convicted came from the public. Was he responsible at all for their deaths or wasn't it rather their judges who were responsible? The fact is that a man was active at the center of this horror whom no one could accuse of a lack of compassion.

Example 4. In the 60s of the last century, the American psychologist Stanley Milgram carried out an experiment. It was a form of quiz. He instructed the test subjects to administer an electric shock for every wrong answer given by a person in another room whom they couldn't see — first a light shock, then an increasingly strong one on a scale of up to 450 volts with every further wrong answer. The experiment started and the subjects increased the voltage. If they had misgivings, they were urged by the experimenter to keep going. And they kept going. Most of them went up to 450 volts. For those on the receiving end it would have been life-threatening if it hadn't been faked.

Milgram changed the test. In the next test groaning and increasingly loud cries of pain in reaction to the electric shocks were played from a tape. A third of the subjects, encouraged by the experimenter, still went up to the highest voltage. When Milgram published the results of his test series, everyone was shocked . . .

These results are still harrowing today. Because the participants behaved ruthlessly but were in no way unfeeling. Asked prior to the experiment to predict what they would do, they couldn't imagine going beyond 150 volts. But as soon as they sat in front of the panel with the buttons, hardly had the process started than most of them felt entitled to give the "maximum penalty". Everything was after all under scientific control and the experimenter would stop the process in time.

Lack of compassion? This was not the case at all. However, our compassion seems to be subject to considerable fluctuation. Whenever we believe in the legitimacy of suffering, we are tempted to make an exception, as if "deserved" suffering didn't earn our pity. We don't need to be callous monsters, but as soon as a state or scientific authority confronts us with their expectations, our moral apparatus is in danger of breaking down. As if the fact that the evil in question is legitimized by some higher authority were excuse enough. Being a compassionate person is thus far from being a guarantee against evil.

Apparently our conscience slips easily into any form that any representative of authority holds up like a coat. In this coat we feel safe — and probably relieved that we've rid ourselves of our responsibility at the same time as our compassion. What's overlooked here is that legitimacy is not in itself a seal of moral approval. No, the compassionate executioner of Paris could have said, I'm not carrying out thousands of illegal sentences. And the participants in the Milgram experiment could have listened to their consciences rather than to the experimenter. Or would that have been asking too much?

Here we can't see where evil begins either. It doesn't seem possible to draw a line between good and evil in reality. The examples cited only prove that we like to toe any official line. Compassion is evidently not a constant, it occurs sporadically and is even compatible with objective evil, as both cases show. As a formula for evil, lack of compassion is thus excluded. But what about hostility?

Example 5. The couple on the fourth floor have always greeted the others cordially on the stairs. Then there is a dispute between them and the other tenants about the garbage cans and since then they haven't been greeting the others on the stairs. They pass them all with stubbornly lowered heads and don't even react when people try greeting them. Everyone, probably the stubborn pair themselves as well, finds the situation unpleasant, but this doesn't change things . . .

Relations have been severed. Because of a trifle, it's true, but the consequences are annoying and everyone suffers from the hostility that has crept into the house. Here injured vanity and pride are involved and finally the line can be drawn exactly: it's the moment where the losers of the garbage can dispute decide to cut themselves off . . . Or isn't that the case at all? Isn't evil also measured by the reaction of the people affected by it? What would be left of the hostility if everybody made light of it and said it's not the end of the world, let them stew in their own juice, we aren't going to let it bother us!

Harmlessness is quite obviously not a fixed variable. What some people take lightly gets under others' skins. Couldn't a good deal of egoism, injured vanity or even hostility also often be attributed to the offended person? Only think of jokes that were not meant to do any harm but were taken badly. Think of the widespread, deplorable tendency to impute bad intentions to others that they never had. Or of angry responses to frank speaking. Here I think of my former prior, Father Paul. Anger and outrage were foreign to him. He had the invaluable gift of not getting angry about anything or anyone, he let evil bounce off him. He would never have thought of breaking off contact after a heated verbal exchange, would not have felt victimized and gone away offended, as people often do — for the simple reason that Prior Paul saw life from the higher vantage point of a person who doesn't take anybody too seriously, least of all himself. So there are also disproportionate reactions. From the perspective of a self-confident, inwardly stable person many things seem harmless which others find aggressive or malicious.

Even not resenting everything would be an effective measure against evil. This approach, however, makes it particularly difficult to draw the line between good and evil. Do we just have to accept that the transition between good and evil is fluid and the point where evil originates cannot be identified? Let us look at the final two examples.

Example 6. The serial killer Peter Kürten, subsequently known as the "Vampire of Düsseldorf", came under the influence of an adult animal abuser as a teenager. Together they killed sheep at night. In the course of his confession, Kürten reported how good just the sight of the flowing blood made him feel.

This was thus the prelude to a horrifying series of murders. It began with the torture and killing of animals and you feel that a change came over him during those nights in the fields. Something was stirring within him. The fact that only animals were involved doesn't make things any less uncanny. Because the young Peter Kürten experienced an unsuspected pleasure by killing the sheep and in future this experience would give his life meaning. His victims would pay for his pleasure with their lives, but he would pay for it with his humanity and his soul. However, the price did not seem too high for him. Kürten was ready to give up his own self.

Example 7. A teacher is showing his class a movie about the resistance fighter Sophie Scholl, her work as a member of a small resistance group against Hitler, her arrest, and her execution. Afterwards he is confronted by grinning faces. Some of the girls are upset, but many of the boys are lolling in their chairs with the sardonic grins of hard-boiled know-alls. They respond to his question by saying, "What a stupid woman. You know how something like that is going to end. Why didn't she go with the flow like all the others?" The teacher is stunned . . .

Is this a sign that they are going to the bad? Not necessarily that they are heading for outright criminality, but doesn't their answer indicate indifference, giving us a foretaste of evil? What's the matter with these boys, one wonders. Can they be appealed to morally at all, or is it quite enough for them to know which way the wind blows? To know how to get away with things unpunished. While at this moment all we have is a consternated teacher and no serious damage has been done, one wonders when people are already taking the line of least resistance at a young age and becoming cunning materialists, what this implies for their personality? Their humanity? In other words, hasn't the damage already been done?

In these two cases, something comes to the fore that was lurking in the background of the other examples. This is the fact that you damage yourself if you only have an eye to your own satisfaction and advantage. The story of the temptation of Jesus already showed that evil always directed against one's own person, even if no one else is affected. Every time the tempter shows us his seductive smile, we are forced to ask ourselves who do I really want to be? What do I expect of myself? How valuable to me is my self-esteem? Am I willing to sacrifice my own self — or would I never go so far as to put my identity at stake in order to gain an advantage? For that's what evil is also about: you damage your soul if you go down that road. And now we're able to answer the question about the line: It runs within us, in our life history, where in course of time an attitude to life has emerged. It runs in our own breast between self-esteem and betrayal of ourselves.

Selling one's soul to the devil . . . Basically that's what everyone who opts for evil is doing. For it's always the same exchange that the tempter offers: you could gain a lot if you could only jump over your moral shadow. What this really means is you'd have to betray something that's of great importance for you, your self-esteem and your identity. You'd have to cross a line on the other side of which you would be a changed person, someone strange to you and whom you would possibly want nothing to do with. There's a good reason why we hesitate in moments of temptation: we feel at this moment that our very self is at stake and ask ourselves whether our identity is negotiable (if our conscience is still intact). And so we've found out something definite about evil after all. It shows its repulsive visage not only to the victim. It presents the same visage to the offender — but only at second glance.

7

Adam and Eve are enlightened

If evil is self-destructive, how can it still be a temptation? After all, we're not that masochistic. No rational beings, one would think, would do that to themselves, voluntarily turn themselves into one of those repulsively ugly devils in the old paintings. Or is there something that makes us indifferent to risking our identity? A primal impulse perhaps, that is stronger than all reason? Or a goal for which no price is too high. I would like to explore this question before we delve further into history.

A primal impulse . . . The first one that occurs to me is the self-preservation instinct. In animals, probably practically all behavior is derived from this, but human beings after all have a special form of self. A self-confident self that yearns for all kinds of things that don't strictly speaking come under self-preservation. If we can't therefore take our examples from the animal world — what about looking at children of a very young age? If there is a primal impulse, it must be most apparent in small children. A primal impulse, it should be noted, which would enable us to come to terms with all the disadvantages of evil.

Children, even infants, can be very mean to each other, there's no doubt about that. But do they have a notion of evil? Or to put it more circumspectly, can they be evil in the sense that we've understood the word so far? In their first years of life they don't distinguish between intention and circumstance, between will and coincidence. They have no idea of freedom and responsibility and they don't even make a distinction between themselves as individuals and the world around them, to say nothing of having a grasp of objective norms and standards. And yet very elementary moral categories seem to emerge quickly — the first of which is a kind of sense of justice, presumably initiated by the fear of being overlooked.

In any case children demand attention, right from the very start. Most of all they want undivided attention, but the next best thing is to be given no less than whoever is competing for this undivided attention. Wanting to be noticed and not left out is how it begins. In no way do they want to feel they are being put at a disadvantage and people who really have lost out in their childhood will find it hard to rid themselves of their jealousy as adults. The inborn "sense of justice" in children is so strong that they will remember for months which sibling received half a chocolate egg more than they did. We might then ask ourselves whether we are actually born disadvantaged? Are we bothered from the beginning by the feeling that we are being deprived? Do we drink in envy with our mothers' milk? This jealously defended insistence on our proper share seems to be simply part of our nature — and the root of our self-confidence. Wanting things, fighting for them, possessing and defending them seems to be what is programmed into us. I'm not giving up this stuffed animal, this is how I am.

Children incidentally fight for and defend things from their second year of life on. Anything tangible can henceforth become a source of dispute. "Wanting to take away a coveted object from someone else is a universal and probably very primal ambition," as the behavioral scientist Eibl-Eiblsfeld notes laconically. And children also defend the place where they're playing at an equally early age. What they possess in the original sense of the word, namely with their bottoms, is the part of the world they have conquered and therefore taboo for everybody else. Whereby even at this age they experience rudimentary stirrings of conscience, a slight doubt about the absolute rightfulness of their actions. In the example I would like to look at, Eiblsfeld observed a one-and-a-half-year-old as he set upon an older playmate who had taken his toy. This brief incident, recorded in detail by Eiblsfeld, went as follows: after his first attempt to push over his rival, the boy stopped and looked inquiringly at his mother who was sitting nearby. It was only when she didn't react that he attacked again and did in fact knock his opponent to the ground, but he gave his mother another searching look when the loser started crying. Apparently he was not entirely comfortable with what he'd done.

> It's worth taking a closer look at this casual incident and ask what we've actually seen. The best answer I can give is that it's an experiment. An experiment that concerns wholly existential matters such as one's own position in the world and the ability to change the world at one's own discretion. Let's look at the way the experiment proceeds.

At the beginning, the hero of this little story realizes that his world is not in order. It's only a detail that bothers him, but it bothers him mightily — although any other detail would disturb him just as much because the world of this one-and-a-half year-old is dominated by a simple either–or principle: either everything is in order or everything is wrong. To his delight, he discovers that it is apparently in his power to rectify things, in other words get his toy back, and — the thing that would give him the most pleasure — at the same time teach the child who is scarcely bigger than himself a lesson. This would even doubly satisfy his sense of justice: he would have defended his possession and in addition punished the malefactor. So at any rate it's worth a try.

However, it's not as simple as that. There's his mother. She complicates this test because she's always tended to prevent any actions in any way associated with violence — our hero vaguely remembers such prohibitions. This is why what he intends to do could lead to a trial of strength — not only with the other boy but, with much more alarming consequences, with his mother. This by no means prevents him from continuing, and then he finds the other boy doesn't fend off his attack. So the experiment starts successfully. Now comes the inquiring look at his mother. She looks aside, he's free to carry on, and then there's the second attack. That's also successful, his rival is knocked down, but just before he can take his toy the loser starts crying. This was not planned, this is awkward, because now at the latest he can expect his mother to intervene — at some point she must notice, which will inevitably result in the termination of the experiment. Although in the event it's the sister of the crying boy who intervenes and comforts her brother. Our hero can nevertheless be happy with his experiment. He dared to do what he did, he explored what was possible, he asserted himself in the area under his control, he restored order, and incidentally scored one over his mother, showing her what he thought of her prohibitions. This was evident. The attempt was certainly worth it.

An experiment, an attempt. Or would anyone start talking about a tempter in this context? Would anyone seriously see evil at work here? Would anyone accuse the defender of his rights of even a lack of compassion — or claim his soul had been damaged in the process? Probably not. Moral categories do not yet apply to this age group. Everything they do is a matter of experimenting, trying things out, and gaining experience — which is necessary and therefore makes them innocent.

Or does it?

Not for the mother. She senses something in her son that she can't accept. Something rebellious. Nothing wicked but an undesirable high-handedness which cannot be countered by what is as yet an inadequately developed sense of responsibility. This still needs to be worked on, there is still quite a lot to be ground in. The time of the innocent experiments will therefore come to an end at some point, play will become reality and the experiments will become serious. And this primal impulse? This behavior familiar from early childhood of fighting for, keeping hold of, and defending things as the essence of one's self — does it vanish too when play becomes reality and the experiments serious? Or does it stay with us forever? And if so, is it still necessary, still innocent?

Desiring to possess, experimenting. It is no coincidence that we also encounter both impulses at the very beginning of the Bible, in the story of Adam and Eve and the so-called Fall of Man. The story which deals with the question of how evil came into the world and actually provides an answer — the most conclusive and satisfactory answer I know.

Of course it's not a factual report from the early history of mankind, so the Fall is therefore not true in the sense of a historical occurrence. Yet this story is true for the reason that it exposes the problematic core of human existence. Because Adam and Eve are us: What they experience, what happens to them is the general fate of mankind that is repeated in the life of every individual. This story is thus a dramatized psychoanalytical text. Having said that, I would first like to tell the story in my own words.

God creates the first two people from the earth, breathes his breath into them, and places them in the Garden of Eden. This garden seems to be an orchard with fruit trees that need looking after and watering; this is one of the tasks of these first people called Adam and Eve and it evidently isn't arduous.

In the middle of this orchard grow two trees of a special kind; they are called the tree of life and the tree of knowledge, or more precisely the knowledge of good and evil. While there are no instructions concerning the tree of life, and Adam and Eve can eat its fruit like that of all the other trees, the tree of knowledge is off-limits, and they are forbidden on pain of punishment to eat the fruit. God has impressed it on Adam that "in the day that you eat of it you shall die," and he respects the prohibition. So does Eve. The relationship of both towards their creator is untroubled, their existence a matter of course.

Until the incident with the serpent. It is described as being crafty and craftily it worms its way in, asking Eve, "Did God say . . ." and soon we think we hear a familiar voice, soon the "why not" from the temptation of Jesus sounds in our ears — why not "command these stones to become loaves of bread . . .?" So now comes the question "Did God say 'You shall not eat from any tree in the garden'?" I can't imagine he did, is implied — casting a gentle doubt on the wisdom of God, more explicit doubt on the friendliness of his intentions and alluding unmistakably to the fact that the serpent knows better and has the people's interests more at heart. Eve, slightly surprised at the strange question, answers truthfully and repeats the divine warning against the tree of the knowledge, not forgetting to mention the threat of death. The serpent immediately seizes on the key word die. "You will not die," it explains to Eve, "When you eat of it your eyes will be opened, and you will be like God, knowing good and evil." Implying that that's precisely what God wouldn't stand for, because God insists on his privileges.

Eve gazes at the tree. The tree of knowledge. It's truly a beautiful tree. The most beautiful in the whole garden with the most tempting fruit. Perhaps the serpent is right? It probably is right. This could be put to the test. And Eve plucks a fruit, bites into it and passes it to Adam, who also can't resist it.

Their deed has an immediate effect, although it's not what they expect. Both realize that they've been naked from the beginning and suddenly they're ashamed of it. What if they were seen in this condition . . .? So they hide themselves when God walks in the garden as usual in the cool of the evening, and only when he calls Adam does he come out and excuse himself. He hadn't want God to see him naked. God is immediately in the picture. Excuses follow; Adam blames Eve, Eve blames the serpent, but it's no use, their time in the Garden of Eden has run out, is irrevocably past. "See, the man has become like one of us" says God to himself. So he drives them out before they can eat from the tree of life as well. And he places cherubim outside the garden and a flaming sword to guard the way to the tree of life . . .

As I said, it's not about historical facts. It's about an essential truth. The Old Testament is a study of human behavior and human abysses based on a wealth of experience and Genesis provides us with a masterpiece in the form of the story of the Fall of Man. I will try to uncover its deeper significance.

There's the Garden of Eden where Adam and Eve are lacking in nothing. Their existence is characterized by everlasting harmony. They are on the best of terms with their creator, they keep away from the tree of the knowledge as a matter of course and don't think anything of it — a prohibition is a prohibition and they live a life of innocence in the happy certainty of enjoying God's undivided attention.

And then the serpent makes its appearance. The casual way it addresses itself to Eve is an achievement in itself. You have admit that no other creature in the animal world would be capable of making such a casual approach; the serpent is convincing in this role like no other being. And then "Did God . . .?" dropped into the conversation and sounding as harmless as the questions with which interrogations start. "Did God say. . .?" — "Yes, what?" ". . . that you shall not eat from any tree in the garden?" And now we get to the heart of the matter. The prohibition. So far Adam and Eve have accepted it, without giving it a second thought. Now Eve, suddenly confronted with it, recapitulates with slight irritation what she knows about the matter and has up to now honestly believed. "No, in general we may eat everything here, but — yes you're right — in the middle of the garden is a tree we're supposed to avoid. Because the fruits are deadly, God said . . . ."

And the serpent exults. Eve has become curious, or at least perplexed. The serpent knows how people function: they dream their lives away, but if you make them aware of something they wake up. Now the trap only has to be sprung. And this is the gist of how the serpent goes about it: "That's what God said? Well, what century are we living in? How can you be so naïve and take everything God says at face value? Of course you won't die if you eat from this tree! Instead you'll be like God and be able to differentiate between good and evil!

This sounds rather fantastic to Eve. Should things be different? Whom should she believe? Eve looks for the tree. She has passed it hundreds of times without noticing it, and now she sees it properly. And this settles it. The rest follows on inevitably from this first conscious perception, triggered by the serpent's crazy revelation that a divine prohibition is negotiable. Eve can't stop thinking about the tree. Yes, it's true that it's beautiful. Its fruit is irresistible. In addition, it's supposed to make you wise. Why didn't she have eyes for this fine specimen of a tree before? The matter deserves investigation . . . She plucks a piece of fruit and bites into it. She lets Adam try it too. And with this evil enters the world.

Evil?

No, something else. Shame enters the world. The previously unfamiliar feeling of being naked. The discovery that one doesn't always automatically know whether one is doing the right thing. Why? Because Adam and Eve have just forfeited the support of God. They can no longer base what they do on his authority. For the first time they've been left to fend for themselves and what happens from now on will show whether they can be responsible for their own behavior. Being naked means feeling one is observed. Being exposed without protection to the gaze of others and constantly living with the fear that any other person will know at a glance one has a bad conscience. This is exactly what the writer of this story describes immediately after the eating of the fruit: Adam and Eve hide from God. They turn a deaf ear to him, because they can no longer endure his searching look. They have learned about responsibility and find it very hard to bear.

So the serpent was right. Adam and Eve have indeed been enlightened. In future they will be able to assess their own behavior. From now on they are capable of moral judgment, have mastered the divine art of recognizing evil, and differentiating it from good. The so-called Fall of Man marks the birth of the conscience — and simultaneously marks the birth of freedom. Because from now on, human beings have the choice, from now on they can and must decide for themselves, and their life history is dependent on their free will. Simple prohibitions are no longer effective. God will no longer be able to count on the obedience of mankind. Human beings have become unpredictable, they have emancipated themselves and become free — their greatest triumph. But at what price? Because everything has its price. For Greeks and Jews alike.

With this question we get to the explosive heart of the story. The price of freedom is the break with God. One can't be had without the other. As long as you lived in harmony with God, evil didn't exist. The moment human beings sunder the bond with God, evil enters, because evil can only become a possibility at all through the renunciation of God. In other words, the birth of the conscience, the birth of freedom, is also the birth of evil. This is the Fall of Man.

But wasn't it an innocent experiment that Eve let herself in for? Wasn't it perfectly correct seen in human terms to take a chance, and risk the existing situation with all its advantages for the possible opportunity of growing as a person? Doesn't the prospect of self-perfection justify stepping over any limits, even disobeying a divine command? It was an attempt, an experiment — and weren't they anyway already on the verge of becoming like God? Weren't they associating with God almost as with an equal, weren't they intimates of the creator? Only one more step. A bit of high-handedness . . .

As you can see, this is a psychological text through and through. An attempt to approach the nature of evil via the nature of man and derive the first appearance of evil in this world from a basic human disposition: the — innocent? — urge to put oneself and the current situation at risk. Rebelling, questioning the existing situation, stepping over limits, experimenting, playing with possibilities. Can't you hear the voice of the unscrupulous stockbroker Gordon

Gekko echoing between the trees of the Garden of Eden, when he cries out in Oliver Stone's movie *Wall Street: Money Never Sleeps,* "Can't you understand? It's not about money, it's about the game."

Yes, this pleasure in experimenting may be innocent, but guilt is frequently a consequence. Human freedom and evil are mutually dependent, and however guilelessly Adam and Eve may have approached their experiment, it's their responsibility. They have innocently become guilty.

And what are the consequences? Once in possession of free will, human beings rise above the rest of creation. Nature is henceforth hostile and the fight between good and evil begins simultaneously with the struggle for survival. This is what will be called culture or civilization. Experimenting will be a mark of human existence in future ... God incidentally seems to take a rather mild view of what has happened, which is surprising given the consequences. In any case Adam and Eve survive — although death has entered the world, it does not occur immediately — and before God drives them out of the garden he not only makes them garments of skins, he also puts them on them himself! Could this indicate that the creator himself considers experimenting to be an innocent impulse? Because the caring gesture of dressing can only mean one thing: human beings can continue to count on God's support if they want it. To me at any rate the moderate reaction of the creator seems appropriate to the tragedy of having innocently become guilty.

Greek mythology also addresses this issue. It also asks how evil came into the world and it is actually always interesting to see the similarities and differences between the Bible and mythology. In this case, however, it is disappointing. The Greek Pandora story doesn't have anything remotely like the complexity and depth of the biblical story of the Fall of Man. Judge for yourselves.

Hephaestos, the god of fire, created a woman of metal whom Zeus liked so much that he brought her to life. Her name was Pandora. She was the first human being, and in the absence of human males married the Titan Epimetheus. At her wedding, Zeus gave her a small container, probably a sealed jug, ordering her never to open it under any circumstances. Pandora kept it and also initially obeyed the prohibition, but one day, overwhelmed with curiosity, she did open it. All the ills and vices escaped from the jug and evil poured over a world that hadn't previously known death, toil or temptation. So the earth became a desolate place . . .

Pandora's box, as it is generally known today, has become the epitome of doom. And as a metaphor it is undoubtedly suitable, but it can't shed any light on the origin of evil. In this story, all the vices and weaknesses come ready packaged, obtained from who knows where by Zeus, and now they only have to be let loose in the world. Interestingly enough it's once again a woman who is responsible for this — out of curiosity, as it says; evidently playful, experimental characteristics are associated more with women. And as in the Bible there is also the idea of an original paradise and the irresistible fascination exerted by the prohibition. What is not touched on at all is the indissoluble connection between free will, responsibility, and innocent guilt. Psychological perspicacity, at any rate, is not much in evidence here.

I would therefore like to make one last comment about Adam and Eve. After the Fall of Man, people are able to differentiate between good and evil. But what they don't learn, what they may possibly never learn, is to distinguish between play and reality. This inability is at any rate just as much a characteristic of the one-and-a-half-year-old hero in the case described at the beginning as of the global players of our days.

8

Breaking the vicious circle

Whether we look at the more anecdotal Pandora myth or the profound psychological and philosophical narrative of Genesis on the Fall of Man, we find that evil comes into the world with a big bang. Before this it was not even present as a possibility and suddenly it's there at the same moment that man becomes conscious of the freedom to step over a limit — and with this all limits. "Yes we can," — nothing sums up the experience of the first human couple better than the encouraging slogan Barack Obama used for his first presidential campaign. But — what does "encouraging" actually mean if this freedom simultaneously creates evil and vice versa, evil simultaneously creates freedom? Shouldn't we then be extremely cautious about how we use our freedom?

What we usually expect from freedom is a more beautiful world and a better life. Over 200 years ago it became the rallying cry of Europe and the rest of the Western world, which is still called the "free" world, and in terms of individual freedom now really is beyond all shadow of a doubt free. Here there is an unshakeable belief in freedom that has only one flaw: it suppresses the risks of freedom. Because it also includes the freedom of the person who becomes a lord over life and death: the freedom of the megalomaniac judge during the French Revolution, the freedom of the murderers under National Socialism or, to cite an example closer to home, the freedom of the thugs in the subway station at night. "Yes we can" — these are stirring words, but would the cry for freedom still sound so inspiring if in the same breath you mentioned the necessary limits and the inevitable hardship of freedom? Under the banner of self-control and responsibility it would probably not attract as many adherents.

Freedom is not the sheer delight the politicians and advertising people would have us believe. It's as ambiguous as evil. After the break with God, it's on the one hand the essential element of human self-development and on the other harbors the risk of every imaginable form of inhumanity. It's therefore misleading to speak, as is common nowadays, of an abuse of freedom — freedom can be abused as little as equality — but you can indeed make naïve, reckless or irresponsible use of it, as Zeus and the ancient Greeks repeatedly observed. And they were not the only ones.

The story of the Fall of Man is followed immediately in Genesis by the account of the fratricide of Abel. I´ll discuss this later on in detail. I'll only say this much for the moment: someone, namely Cain, feels disadvantaged by God. The struggle for existence is now in full swing and Cain insists on the same right to success as his brother Abel. But this is evidently what he doesn't have. Abel is doing much better than he is in the race for worldly goods and we know how uncompromisingly small children insist on their share of the world — I'm holding onto my stuffed toy, that's how I am. In this case Cain, furious and full of jealousy, slays his brother Abel because he's unable to tolerate the alleged injustice of God a moment longer. The first action after the Fall is the disposal of a rival.

With this Genesis arrives directly at the second primal impulse, which carries no less weight than the first one, the pleasure in experimenting: the impulse to establish and assert yourself in the world, to secure your share of the world and make as many as possible of the things in it your own. In other words the pursuit of power and ownership. Although in the Bible this impulse is basically made to look as harmless as the yearning for freedom and the pleasure in experimenting; after all, from the beginning God himself orders human beings to "Fill the earth and subdue it and have dominion . . ." In other words: Divide it up between you and use it for your purposes, put your mark on it.

It looks as though man is predestined to chase after territory and possessions just as he is predestined to freedom. The thirst for power is not wicked in itself, but it is just as risky as freedom. We must be able to cope with both impulses, because they can both only lead to good when they are kept under control.

And with this we come back to the question that occupied us in the sixth chapter: who or what is to blame for evil? Or put differently: can we expect any progress with respect to passion versus reason in the two thousand years we still have to explore?

Now that the much-vaunted passions have taken more concrete shape in the ancient world, it will be easier to assess the problem. You can imagine how explosive the mixture will be when the unrestrained pursuit of power comes up against the unfettered urge for freedom; you can positively see how this explosive charge, once ignited, will erupt in a firework of egocentrism, ruthlessness, greed, violence, and cruelty. And you can understand why all the attempts to find a solution up to now have begun with reason and self-control — this explosive charge must not explode, it must be defused in time otherwise the untamed horses of passion will gallop off with everyone involved.

A highly explosive situation of this nature existed in the Roman province of Palestine before the first millennium AD. Many Jews saw the Roman occupying power as the epitome of evil and tried to seal themselves off from the oppressor culturally or turn to armed resistance. In this context, a man proclaimed his message with whom I would like to start the second part of my tour of history: Jesus of Nazareth.

If I may put it like this: with Jesus we experience the second big bang, namely an unheard-of new concept of human behavior. The man from Nazareth is far more radical than everyone who has spoken on this issue before or after him. He's not a moralist. He doesn't call the people to order. He's a revolutionary. He turns all social values on their head, he turns the tables, and when the Jewish and Roman authorities later execute him in a joint action as a blasphemer or a rebel, respectively, we can safely use a more modern word for this: cultural revolutionary. For that's what he had in mind: a cultural revolution.

Jesus completely redefines the freedom of man and goes far beyond free will in the process. His freedom means departure from all the conventional standards of happiness and success, from traditional bonds, from laws and regulations, from all the limitations of conventional imagery as well as from the imperious impulses of the natural self-preservation drive. Jesus says, if human beings achieve inner autonomy, they could detach themselves from all these dependencies. With him, this autonomy is achieved to such a high degree that at the end he overcomes his own fear of death and provokes his execution. What is the nature of this autonomy?

It has little to do with self-control. Rather it is the exact opposite, namely release, letting go, the deepest inner relaxation; with this I am reminded again of the painters' depiction of God that radiates precisely this sovereignty of a person in a state of complete autonomy. And this state cannot be achieved by being brought to reason through a suitable upbringing and a proper educational process, as Plato had his Socrates think. Nor is this form of controlled dispassion the object at all. Jesus himself was anything but dispassionate — he was considered by many to be mad or possessed and his disciples were repeatedly exposed to his temperamental nature. No, this autonomy arises from a complete inner freedom, absolute independence from all social, cultural, and religious constraints, even from the drives of human nature and the relentless claims of the ego. And all it is based on is an unconditional or childlike trust in God, because the intimate, familiar approach to God maintained by Jesus makes the whole world appear in a different light. It leads us to learn to see the world through the eyes of God and that means through the eyes of love.

Love is the key word. But this love has nothing pathetic, nothing dramatic about it. It is the inconspicuous love, geared to the practical needs of humanity, of the person who inwardly listens to the voice of God and acts according to his will. For Jesus this neighborly love expresses the moral independence of the autonomous human being. In his teachings, reason can only be spoken of in a higher sense of the word. He exposes as insignificant and absurd the normal security- and efficiency-thinking which we find so undeniably reasonable today — as is also shown in the story of the temptation. His reason is contrary to everything usually understood by it; it expresses itself in a kind of holy levity. Escape from the routine of everyday life, he urges his audience, put the constant thoughts about the future out of your mind, stop worrying and planning all the time, and take the birds as your example — "they neither sow nor reap nor gather into barns and yet your heavenly father feeds them."

So here is somebody who is taking issue with reflexes that others consider natural and innate and therefore reasonable. No, Jesus says, these reflexes may follow ingrained patterns of behavior but they prove only that you're blindly following the rules of society like everyone else. This becomes even clearer in his ethics as summarized by the Evangelist Matthew in the Sermon on the Mount.

Their aim is to break the vicious circle of evil. But not by fighting it, because resistance is entirely in line with the logic of evil — this is after all how it's perpetuated, repaying like with like. Nor do his ethics require that you keep your head down and dumbly submit to evil. Instead Jesus recommends going on the offensive: acting rather than merely reacting, taking the initiative, confronting evil, and paradoxically meeting it with kindness, gentleness, and peacefulness. Taking the wind out of evil's sails, rendering it ineffective, to some extent causing it to implode before it explodes. This is precisely what is meant by the famous phrase from the Sermon on the Mount: turn the other cheek.

This is an entirely new approach. Even Asian philosophies of that time, for example the Tao, teach their followers not to resist evil, and say it's wiser not to leave oneself too open to the adversities of life. When Jesus encourages people to respond when evil attacks by counterattacking with good, this isn't an appeasement measure, but practical love offered in advance, an unconditional expression of friendship, as it were. But what would be gained by it?

A great deal, and for everyone concerned. First the victims would get back their sovereignty if they overcame evil with the power of love and in this way left it behind them. On the other hand, the perpetrators would keep their dignity, because the minute a victim doesn't react as expected, they regain their freedom of decision — and suddenly they have to reconsider their behavior, suddenly they've been given the opportunity to change their minds. They probably won't always do so. But if they did, the vicious circle would be broken and the iron rule that evil continuously begets evil invalidated. The paradoxical strategy of Jesus, overcoming evil with good, does have considerable merit. It has only one drawback: it's extremely challenging.

Because it requires rejection of all the popular ideas of justice and nullifies the usual reasoning that you are due this and that, that this is what you deserve and this is what the other person deserves. Jesus doesn't reckon up. He wants nothing to do with a balanced account of giving and taking. He forgives seven times seventy times, even if the other person doesn't forgive a single time. Whoever practices such a radical form of neighborly love must do this quite independently of the evil intentions of others. The ethics of Jesus require the absolute moral autonomy of the individual and, you might ask whether he's trying to overturn the laws of the world. Can anybody be so disciplined?

In fact this strategy requires people who are willing to fully reorient and completely redefine themselves. People who no longer obey the unwritten laws of society, who no longer participate in the poker game for power and money, who are tired of the permanent desire to win and triumph, who no longer fight for the best seats in the arena of life. In short: people who understand the difference between an enviable life and a happy life. Jesus thus mainly addresses the underprivileged. This is why the poor are blessed, those who are nothing in this world and never will be, the ones who long for quite another kind of happiness and quite different conditions. In the relationship with God nobody misses out, says Jesus. As sons and daughters of the heavenly father we are all the same. Whoever maintains this relationship will learn over time to look at the world through the eyes of love. And that's all that's needed, if the human race wants at some point to escape the vicious circle of evil.

I've gone into so much detail about the contribution of Jesus because no teacher of mankind tackled the problem of evil as boldly as he did. Or, incidentally, as optimistically. Who else has credited people with being able to change so radically — without the warnings of Bautzen, Gulag or concentration camps? Who else has expected us to begin with ourselves and only with ourselves in the process of transforming the world? Who else has held out the prospect of such sovereignty and inner freedom — and simultaneously so relentlessly confronted us with our own responsibility? Of course everything is only possible, only conceivable in the closest most trusting relationship with God, but a strong belief in man also speaks out of his teaching.

Nevertheless, the people around him soon realized the dimensions of his project. Was it his intention to heal the break with God? Was it possibly his destiny to revoke the curse of the Fall of Man, the connection of freedom with evil? Wasn't it obvious to see in him the redeemer, the Son of God? Over the next few centuries, the teaching of Jesus — and the faith in him — developed a tremendous dynamic, spreading through the entire Roman Empire in a wide variety of manifestations, from ascetic hermits and cloistered monastics to the parishes of ordinary citizens, all of which have one thing in common: the conviction that one day everyone will have to answer for their lives at the Last Judgment. Individual responsibility is beyond question. The only remaining refuge of evil is now in fact the soul of man.

Or is it?

What about the devil? What about Satan and his army of demons?

That brings us once again to the dramatic side of evil and the human need to transfer psychological conflicts to an invisible, or even better, a visible world. And what screams louder for a stage and clearly identifiable actors than the eternal, daily struggle waged between good and evil. The desire to bring this struggle into the world of the imagination is very old and found everywhere on earth. Even in the ancient world, the Jews equipped the kingdom of God with faces and figures, celestial beings, ministering spirits, hierarchically ordered, who were continuously underway on behalf of their Lord, unless their assigned duty was to praise God. And at the time of Jesus the realm of evil had long been similarly organized: as a crowd of demons, over whom Satan and Beelzebub presided as God's adversaries.

But we mustn't think these beings have the same reality as things in the visible world. Demons are forces which can take possession of the soul, they are bad energies, which manifest as psychological or even physical disorders. The entire drama happens on an intellectual level, which doesn't make it any less real. But how is it possible to speak about psychological processes as long as there is no psychoanalytical vocabulary? You narrate. You clothe findings in pictures and stories. You show the battle of good and evil on a stage that extends from heaven to hell — always taking care to speak in symbols and allegories. Only in the late Middle Ages does the devil acquire a frightening presence in Europe and become a part of the real world as the devil incarnate — you only have to think of the inkwell Martin Luther is said to have thrown at him. This development is partly attributable to a failure of the church, which abetted such vulgar beliefs, and partly to ancient folklore. For nothing has inflamed the imagination as much as evil, at all times and in all places.

As far as I can judge, all the cultures of the earth have a subterranean and a celestial world, evil and good spirits, and throughout the ages we see people at work trying to bring evil under their control to use its power for their own purposes or to fend it off and render it harmless. An army of magicians, shamans, priests is busy with invocation rituals and making amulets in a world where evil intention can be seen in every happenstance, accident and stroke of fate, and is hence practically omnipresent. Under such circumstances, the dividing wall between the world of humans beings and spirits is very thin, and demons or devils can easily move from one to the other. It was to the credit of the church that it banished the haunting, arbitrarily operating and frightening spirit world from the minds of the people and condemned as it as superstition. It was a scandal that the church then revived this dark world in the late Middle Ages.

Satan would provide material for a whole chapter. If only because the impact of Christianity is based to a large degree on pictorial representations and therefore repeatedly required an embodiment of evil — Christianity is eminently a religion of artists and often painters were the more influential theologians. Since we will encounter Satan again, I will only indicate here the most dramatic escalation of the struggle between good and evil that we know: the Apocalypse. The last book of the Bible contains gruesome visions of a cosmic showdown between God and the devil, whose power is lost forever at the Last Judgment. The Apocalypse dashes all hopes that evil could basically be defeated in the way Jesus taught.

9

In search of innocence

In the fight against evil, should we start with the individual, in other words expect individuals to put themselves in order, in the hope that in their reformed state they will have a humanizing effect on society as a whole? This would be the ethical strategy of Christianity. Or should we start with the state and the constitution, first putting the world in order, and hope this will have a domesticating or similarly humanizing effect on the individual? This strategy would correspond to the Greco-Roman tradition.

Europe in the Middle Ages had both traditions in its repertoire. Although it was Christian, its theologians and philosophers tended to value reason in a similar way to the thinkers of the ancient world. An enviably rich heritage, one might say, and perhaps expectations were never higher: if you were to combine the two strategies, if you could produce a synthesis of Christian and Greek ideas — would you not come closer than ever before to the ideal situation? The great thinkers of the Middle Ages worked on this project with the goal of erecting a double bulwark against evil: the outside world was to be stably and permanently ordered, while the individual was expected to have a heightened awareness of responsibility and guilt.

Towards the end of the Middle Ages, the project came to a standstill. Were the expectations too high? Were the Christian ideals only too evidently ridiculed by the reality? From then on, in increasingly rapid succession, European thinkers produced ideas about where the cause of all evil was to be sought and how moral decay could be redressed. Ideas which fluctuated strangely from one extreme to the other. Phases of euphoria when people were credited with being able to rise far above themselves alternated with periods of gloomy pessimism when man was considered a hopeless case, ripe for the next flood, one might almost say. I would like to give a few examples of this development.

The new thinking made its first appearance in Italy during the Renaissance. For centuries, man was viewed as a sinner in need of redemption. But when you now look at the famous *Oration on the Dignity of Man* by Pico della Mirandola (1463-94), you cannot believe your eyes: in almost elegiac words, the Italian describes man as having the potential to be a fascinating, indefinable being, not bound to any role or stage of development, endlessly changeable and capable of anything, from becoming like God to "descend to the lower, brutish forms of life."

Here we are experiencing a moment when, after a long time, the moral compass needle is pointing in a new direction. How can I win God for myself? That is the core question of human existence according to Christianity. Pico della Mirandola rephrases this. He asks himself how can he become as similar as possible to God. And his answer is: not through moral effort. Not by mobilizing all his spiritual powers against evil. But by imitating God as the creator. By developing his intellectual and creative potential. By not accepting the world as he finds it, like animals do, but by ordering it more sensibly to meet his own needs. This is a proactive concept. It sets enormous energies free. Suddenly all human conditions become raw material for a new type of person, who feels the power within himself or herself to continue the divine work of creation. And not only the power, but the duty too.

Moral inhibitions are more likely to interfere with this task "descend[ing] to the lower, brutish forms of life . . ." doesn't mean the danger of becoming an unprincipled and unscrupulous villain (an impressive number of which were produced during Renaissance). It means the descent into an irrational and passive state that robs us of our creativity. The alternatives are no longer saint or sinner, but demigod or animal. According to Pico della

Mirandola, neither faith nor even love decide the path a person will follow — this is determined by the improvement of his or her reason or the equally feasible loss of it.

Two centuries later the animal has grown fangs. The Englishman Thomas Hobbes (1588–1679) is deeply pessimistic when he describes the normal state of the world as a war of all against all and compares human beings in this condition to wolves. There is no more talk of demigods, or of the fantastic development possibilities of man. In their blind egoism, Hobbes wrote, the people would "use violence to make themselves masters of other men's persons, wives, children and cattle . . . . defend them . . . [or to take their revenge] for trifles, as a word, a smile, a different opinion, and any other sign of undervalue. Their lives are therefore solitary, poor, nasty, brutish and short." In a word, man has failed.

A damning judgment and the worst thing about it is that the individual can't change a thing. Everyone is a dwarf with respect to moral stature — or a wolf. In order to protect people from themselves, they must be taken into custody, or to put it more precisely, only in the care of a powerful state will the individual of necessity become a reasonable being. Would that be the solution — the state, equipped with every instrument of power, functioning like a huge watchdog, like a strict guardian? Hobbes doesn't of course design his state like a prison, because it also guarantees the citizens rights — but what we have here is in any case a vote of no confidence in human nature. The innocent reason-euphoria of the Renaissance has vanished, and there is no more talk of the great hope Jesus invested in man. No, says Hobbes, man is not actually evil. Just completely asocial.

A century later someone else strikes a totally different note, the Frenchman Jean-Jacques Rousseau (1712-78). He locates the cause of all moral depravity not in human nature, but, of all places, in civilization. Whereas his enlightened contemporaries think it was precisely civilization that was the seat of reason and hence moral progress! This is wrong, says Rousseau. Because civilization produces nothing but competitiveness and selfishness, and the result is simply shocking: people hate, betray, defame, and murder each other. In a word, the civilized person is evil.

No preacher of repentance could have put it better. And this voice of indignant disappointment now prevails for quite a time. The human species has probably never been so poorly rated before. What's to be done?

Rousseau advocates freeing people from the straitjacket of civilization. The original moral instinct inherent in people in their formerly natural existence must be revived — the noble savage is his ideal, a dreamy harmless narcissist, innocence incarnate. Should human beings now return to the animal kingdom? In a letter to Rousseau, Voltaire says mockingly, "Reading your book makes me want to walk around on all fours." This, as is usual with Voltaire, is exaggerated, but it hits the nail on the head. Because Rousseau's rescue plan for human beings is nothing less than a romantic reversal of the biblical story of Paradise. He wants to undo the Fall of Man. He wants to return to the state in which human beings are still ignorant of their freedom and live in the same innocent state as animals.

The leaders of the Enlightenment can't be dissuaded by Rousseau from their belief in reason and civilization. But even they agree that human beings can't remain in their present state and must be worked on if they don't improve themselves voluntarily. But their bitterness over the pitiful drama of mankind is directed against the church. Too much is probably expected of it, and now one mustn't expect anything more — it has had its time but now this is now over. They counter Rousseau's pessimism about civilization with the familiar optimism that conditions will improve fundamentally as soon as man finally learned to behave like a rational being. And once again evil is identical with thoughtlessness and ignorance, in other words with the absence of enlightenment.

Illuminating the world with the fire of reason after centuries of

Christian darkness — this is the vision that inspires the thinkers of the 19th century. They work ceaselessly to fundamentally improve the condition of the human race, with an eye to the final reward of liberty, equality, fraternity. In the meantime audacious dreams, both pleasant and terrible, anticipate the actual success.

For Heinrich Heine (1797–1856), for example, the world of the future human being who's been brought to reason takes the form of a modern Greek paradise. The new paradise will more or less come to pass of its own accord as soon as Christianity with its dogmas and pious rules comes to an end and the human race at last innocently enjoys what was previously forbidden or frowned upon. We'll finally be transformed into an assembly of lovable gods who sing their own praises with serene complacency. This liberated human race will not know about sin, simply because after the collapse of the church nobody will speak about sin and evil will therefore have disappeared without more ado.

A dream, as I've said, not a serious forecast, because here Heine is employing a simple sleight of hand. The logic behind his serene utopia is that where there is no judge, there is no crime. As if you only have to close your eyes to the existence of evil and it will disappear. As poetically naïve as this is — one of the most important philosophers of the 19th century takes a similar approach, but with a different result.

Friedrich Nietzsche (1844–1900) dreamed of a type of human being who only obeys his own will and exclusively acts at his own discretion. No prohibitions exist for this Superman, as Nietzsche calls him. He is a creature who listens to no one and is as autonomous as Jesus Christ originally suggested his followers could be, but beholden to no one, neither God nor man, completely free of responsibility and thus completely irresponsible. Why should we think that the world of this liberated Superman would be any better? Only someone who believes like Nietzsche that one could banish evil from the world along with moral law can understand this.

After all, Nietzsche proceeds in his daring speculation from a realistic assessment of the situation: after the death of God, as he calls the triumph of rationalist thinking, human beings can no longer live as before. All orientation will be lost, all moral principles destroyed, they will be adrift like a ship on the high seas without navigation instruments. Human beings in their present form are much too poorly equipped to give themselves a new moral order, they are weaklings and all that remains to them is to rise far above themselves and become similar to gods. In this fundamentally new state, however, Nietzsche is confident that through their own willpower people will force evil back to the place from which it was evoked by Adam and Eve.

One can sense how the religious energies that have been released look for new outlets in the 19th century and create new worldly paradises, but you can also feel a growing perplexity, mixed with despair. Judging by their halting progress through history up until now, it seems evident that human beings can't cope with evil. But what conclusion should we draw from this? That this is how human beings are and they can't be any different? That God had been right with his resigned conclusion after the flood that man was ". . . evil from youth?" Impossible. This one can't accept as a rational being. It must be possible to do something. So is it better to maintain a naïve and unrealistic image of man like Heinrich Heine with his peaceful and cheerful god-men and Rousseau with his noble savage? Better to ask people to shed their old, ugly skin and reinvent themselves like Nietzsche's Superman? But how far can man actually rise beyond himself? And is he at all interested in doing so?

The fact is that reason is still not working any miracles. And then along comes Sigmund Freud (1856–1939), who claims that the human consciousness in which the thinkers of the Enlightenment had placed their hopes is only apparently rational. In reality it is simmering beneath the smooth surface. Unconscious conflicts affect all our thoughts and actions and strictly speaking we are constantly faced with the irrational behavior of irrational beings. All we can do is to explore the human heart as described by the poet of Psalm 139, breaking through the surface to expose the deeper layers of the soul in order to reach the source of evil.

Sigmund Freud and others get to work and it is no surprise to find that aggressive impulses have a life of their own unchecked by reason. Nothing is controlled rationally and everything is directed from behind the scenes by a host of unconscious motives, led by sexuality. Nevertheless, Freud's bad news is accompanied by the faint hope that this witches' coven may to some extent be controlled if it is made accessible to reason. And thus we have arrived after a long journey back at the point reached by the ancient Jews more than 2000 years ago: self-exploration and illumination of the most hidden corners of the heart. But this time with psychoanalysis in the role of God.

It's hard not to be discouraged by the above examples of human thinking. What fruits has the struggle against evil borne, what was the use of constantly devising new ethical strategies? In view of the failure of this struggle, isn't it more a case of desperate attempts rather than strategies? There's nothing that seems to help permanently against evil and human beings are constantly trying to force back evil, or at least contain it. Always with the same indifferent success, so that the nasty suspicion arises that evil might ultimately be fulfilling a meaningful function; it might be the hated but essential driving force, it might to some extent be the productive thorn in the flesh of mankind that can range from unpleasant to terrible, but is overall precisely the energy to which we owe all intellectual development and all progress . . .

Only, of course, if you don't resign yourself to it. Nor does anyone do so intentionally. From the 18th century on, we even experience a growing nervousness, the increasing impatience of intellectual people with the rest of mankind, which can extend to contempt as with Hobbes, Rousseau and Nietzsche — it is as if evil has in the meantime gained the upper hand in the shape of decadence and brutalization so that no time is to be lost. But assuming this is not based on a progressive decline of morals, the only other possible explanation is deep disappointment in the church. In this case it isn't mankind that has failed, but Christianity, and the disappointment is in proportion to the high moral claim of its teaching.

For in no other period or place was the ethical benchmark as high as in Christian Europe — which must have made the meager results all the more despairing. Had the church simply taken on too much? Was it not now time to disempower and drive out the priests with their delusions of neighborly love and bliss? As if they simply couldn't look at the wretched spectacle of life any more, philosophers and scientists assumed the role of priests and simply claimed to be responsible for the future moral orientation of the human race. This claim was as exclusive as the claim of the church in the past and fierce rivalry was the result: science and faith would face each other unforgivingly from now on. The symbiosis between the Christian and Greek path had failed.

One crucial point was overlooked by the participants in this dispute: the pioneers of a new, absolutely rationally organized world were profoundly shaped by Christianity. They had embraced its high ethical values and most importantly inherited its awareness of responsibility. The extent of their disappointment identified them basically as believers with great moral sensitivity, their zeal confirmed their Christian sense of responsibility and their occasionally deadly seriousness showed that they would not be satisfied with less than Christianity. The salvation of man was still on the agenda. Hence their visions of a renewed human race — harmless and serene as with Heine, terrifying as with Nietzsche, a community of equals as with Marx. And in the background the Viennese psychoanalyst Sigmund Freud with his bitter message that all this probably wouldn't help.

It didn't help simply because people could no longer even agree on a major strategy against evil. In the 19th and 20th centuries, Europe was flooded with a stream of theories, utopias, ideologies, and philosophies of life, all of which plundered the weakened body of Christianity, tearing out what looked useful, underpinning the spoils with pseudo-scientific arguments and selling the whole as a product of reason. Does this mean the synthesis succeeded? At most as a farce. At most to the extent that you can no longer distinguish between the rational and the theological because reason is impregnated with religion and the utopian is cloaked in reason. And with this we have arrived in the present.

10

Did the serpent promise too much?

For some time I've been noticing a strange development. During a discussion, someone finds the furious pace at which our world is changing alarming and perhaps comments critically on the compulsive optimization and restructuring, the jettisoning of everything before any measure has been given time to prove its worth, and someone else immediately replies that nobody can stop progress, and that's a good thing. Change is a basic principle of existence, standstill would be the death of us. But the same people who have just evoked permanent change as a law of existence go on the defensive as soon as moral decay is mentioned. No, they say then, that's nothing new. Appearances are deceptive. Every generation has complained about this state of affairs, nothing's changed since Adam and Eve, it's always been like this.

This takes one aback. A basic principle of existence with exceptions? And evil is the one thing that's apparently not affected by tempestuous change? However, this is probably not a logical but an emotional response, because one thing can be said with certainty: in our day this question touches a nerve. It attacks the belief in progress, and that is taboo, progress must be beyond all doubt. Only a heretic would query its price, because our confidence is founded on progress. For this reason it can't be considered evil. And for this reason we certainly don't want to see social changes in terms of decline. The belief in progress doesn't mix with brutalization and decadence; here it's advisable to deny any influence on morals and better to believe in ineradicable evil which continues to exist through the ages and is not linked to the present. Anything else would be disturbing. Nothing is more frowned upon than cultural pessimism.

Yet this pessimism has been ruling unchallenged for a long time. Everywhere, in fact, where writers and journalists, screenwriters and movie directors take a serious look at the future. What they present to us in their books and movies is fed without exception by gloomy forebodings, depressing visions of a soulless, inhuman world in a state of ruin and decay, all of it reflecting the anxiety that human beings might lose control of things, that frightening developments might take on a life of their own and it may no longer be possible to curb destructive forces. Meanwhile the future seems to be entirely black and this makes me wonder. It seems to be a sign of our times that hope has completely disappeared from our visions of the future. People apparently no longer ask whether things couldn't perhaps change for the better. How has that come about?

Perhaps we are exhausted. Maybe resignation is also a lesson of history, after we've tried everything in the struggle against evil and experienced massive upheavals in the process — mostly with the same mediocre success, and sometimes with harrowing results. "The huge intellectual efforts made to understand our situation and how it could develop haven't been based on hope for a long time," says the writer Martin Mosebach, "but reveal a . . . helplessness tinged with fear."

But it's not only the results that are disappointing. According to the sobering findings of the previous chapters, there's not even been a successful diagnosis. One doctor after the other bends over the patient called the human race, examines him — albeit thoroughly — determines the cause of the disease, rejects the diagnoses of his predecessors and prescribes a new treatment. The condition of the patient never gets better, and when we look at the last century, the 20th, we're even faced with the fact that the patient has never been in such a bad state as this. In this period there was a positive explosion of evil, with murderous energies released on an unprecedented scale. According to the Black Book of Communism, about 100 million deaths from execution and starvation and through revolutions, wars, and civil wars can be attributed to an ideology which was dedicated to the liberation of mankind. Through the Holocaust and World War Two, National Socialism was responsible for 50 million deaths. And added to this are the ten million deaths during World War One whose battles have become the epitome of horror. It's not surprising we're exhausted.

For the sake of clarity, I would like to list everything that has been pinpointed down the ages as the cause of evil by the people of our cultural sphere. This list is far from complete, but it includes more recent findings that I've not mentioned so far. The result is as follows:

- Fate (ancient Greeks)
- Ungodliness (ancient Jews)
- The passions (ancient Greeks)
- Lack of faith (Jesus Christ — put very simply)
- Irrationality (the Renaissance)
- Egoism (Thomas Hobbes)
- Civilization (Jean-Jacques Rousseau)
- Social inequality (the Enlightenment)
- Christianity/the church (also the Enlightenment)
- The aristocracy (French Revolution)
- Capitalism (Karl Marx)
- The wretchedness of man (Friedrich Nietzsche)
- Man's basically irrational structure (psychoanalysis)
- The Jews (National Socialism)
- Our repressive society (the 1968 generation)
- The suppression of instincts (Arno Plack)
- Intolerance (political correctness)

• A malformation of the anterior lobe of the brain (neuroscience)

In other words, hardly anything has been left out. In the last 200 years, the range of explanations for evil has increased by leaps and bounds, resulting in utter confusion. Aside from that, the list frequently shocks you because some diagnoses are anything but harmless, purely theoretical attempts at interpretation. Instead they themselves contain the seeds of evil, because in order to eradicate evil they instigate the eradication of people, in as great a number as possible. It's only a small step from personified evil to the burning of heretics and witches, to the bloodthirsty French Revolution, the concentration camps of the communists and National Socialists and the terror of the Baader-Meinhof gang; we then ask ourselves with horror whether it isn't perhaps precisely an excess of moral zeal, of moral certainty, that helps evil win its most gruesome victories. Must mankind really learn the lesson of the flood repeatedly — does it take only one survivor for the whole destructive activity to have been in vain? In any case, we can now add the next, particularly disastrous cause of evil to our list: it can also arise from the determination to be good.

The main reason for this may be that in the eyes of their proponents, high ideals justify all victims and suffering, and the abolition of evil is undoubtedly a high ideal. History provides examples of this in abundance, and in the last century in particular, good intentions were the driving force for murder on a massive scale. To mention an already half-forgotten incident, at the end of the 1970s, the Khmer Rouge in Cambodia set out to liberate their society from evil and in this way killed a quarter of the population. The Frenchman François Bizot had witnessed the extensive killing firsthand as a camp prisoner and reported later that he remembered the camp commander as a thoughtful person, a serious seeker of truth, and a fanatical believer in justice. This man, however, had about 40,000 people on his conscience. The best example of moral terrorism, however, is Maximilien Robespierre (1758-94), the mastermind of the French Revolution. Outlining his program at the beginning of the Revolution he said, "We want to substitute people who are magnanimous, powerful, and happy for people who are kindly, frivolous, and miserable." Did anyone at the time stumble over the word "substitute"? Robespierre only got as far as beheading people. His companion Saint Just explained cynically that "In order for justice to prevail tomorrow, we are forced to be unjust today."

Apparently the highest ideals can also cause the greatest disaster, as if people in a state of moral exhilaration react with murderous irritability to everything that bothers them in their contemporaries. In this context, the Russian novelist M. Ageyev compares the human soul to a swing, which, when strongly pushed in the direction of humanity, swings back just as violently towards inhumanity. Look at in this way, ideals are something we should beware of. However the question is whether with a total absence of ideals we would be in danger of falling into a state of moral lethargy.

In our time, the large number of diagnoses also has a surprising effect: we can practically choose today which devil has ridden us or is riding us. And now a very interesting development can be observed. Given the option, people are most likely to choose the devil who weighs upon them the least, an anonymous devil contained in objective conditions, the repressive society, the unjust economic system, the wrong education or our basic biological make-up. These are powerful, overpowering instances, in the face of which individual responsibility fades into insignificance, and if we're looking for a single term that covers them all, no better word occurs to me than fate.

So does this take us back to where we started? Where it all began 3,000 years ago? We can't quite reject this idea out-of-hand. Guilt and consciousness of guilt are already being dismissed as a diabolical invention of the church, not even the parish priest talks about sin, and you now get disapproving looks if you hint at the dangerousness of the human race. All of a sudden a lot seems to be explicable, excusable, as a result of a dreadful childhood, in response to societal injustice — you could almost see this as a modern form of fatalism. But before we talk of having taken a step backwards and reverted to old patterns of thinking, we should ask whether fate mightn't perhaps be bringing us closer to the truth about evil. Aren't we in fact in every respect products of our environment, also in terms of our consciousness of injustice? Don't we all see the world through the lens of our education, milieu, culture, and time? In short, didn't the serpent possibly promise too much when it lured Eve with the prospect of being able to distinguish between good and evil as precisely as God?

Slavery is a good example of the power of conditions. Human trafficking as it was commonly practiced from the 17th to the 19th centuries. Common because nobody took exception to the capturing of Africans in their home countries, transporting them forcibly to the coast, cramming them under inhuman conditions into ships, ferrying them in this state for weeks across the Atlantic and finally selling them like goods and exploiting them on plantations as workers without rights. There was general concurrence with what was going on. Apparently no one felt guilty about it. Everyone was apparently acting in good faith, the slave hunters, the ship's chandlers, and captains, the dealers and buyers in the slave markets, the plantation landowners — it was a widespread practice, neither forbidden by law nor at all morally reprehensible. Everyone felt they were in the right and it was as if a new paradise had been created, inhabited by innocents to whom good and evil were as meaningless as they were to Adam and Eve before the Fall of Man. But when the consciousness of injustice is dormant, when the conscience sees no reason to intervene, where then is evil? It doesn't appear, it doesn't exist at all. There is no devil riding anyone anywhere. Nobody is responsible, everybody is innocent, everybody is a child of his or her time and culture, a product of the environment, an innocent whose contact with evil turns it into something normal, approved and therefore good.

So must we assume that evil can make itself invisible? That it can withdraw completely behind a smokescreen of law and order, custom and practice, normality and necessity and stay there undetected for centuries? But can we talk of evil at all if the circumstances don't give rise to a bad conscience? If everyone involved merely perceives a network of legitimate profit interests, a reasonable, excellently organized economic system? Doesn't this rule out moral judgment of the perpetrators?

Looked at in this way, there's a lot to be said for the assumption that the true refuge of evil is to be sought in our overall surroundings, not in the soul of the individual. Especially since there are many other similar cases: the exploitation of the Indios in the gold mines of Peru and the extremely cruel medieval penal system — and perhaps even the guards in the concentration camps were convinced that they were doing what was right and necessary. In such cases, therefore, the political and economic structures ought to be changed as well, possibly by force, to wake people from their delusion of innocence. Under the new humane conditions, people will see reason of their own accord.

So a great deal has indeed changed since Adam and Eve. What was good yesterday can be bad tomorrow and vice versa. Is evil therefore relative, depending on the time, place, culture, and perspective? All development workers would confirm this. They go out into the world to initiate noble sociopolitical projects, inspired by Western ideals, only to find that our morals meet with incomprehension elsewhere, and conversely to discover that outside Europe many things we find quite intolerable are compatible with the prevailing sense of justice. Long before them, Christian missionaries and explorers had exactly the same experience. Many travel reports from the past reflect shock at the merciless way in which people in far countries were treated, while others in turn admire the gentle mores of foreign peoples. Did the serpent really promise too much? Or have we become like God — but in spite of this not much wiser?

Eventually, however, evil emerges from the backdrop of normality. Eventually there's a change in the prevailing moral mood without the upheaval of a revolution and the generally accepted evil turns into generally rejected evil. This can take a long time — in the case of slavery it took about 250 years — and it can be uncanny and frightening how long it takes for our eyes to be opened. But the day comes when we're shocked to realize that we've done evil things with a good conscience, and what has been legal for decades and centuries is now branded as barbarism. Even under the conditions of previous eras, moral progress was made, and the belief in the omnipotence of conditions was thus also refuted.

Because if we were products of our environment there would be no need for change. We would then be a docile flock and it would go on like this for all eternity. However, the power of conditions is apparently not stronger than the conscience after all. Yes, it is difficult to go against the tide of a highly promising development, it's sometimes as hard as it is to withstand an avalanche. Nobody thinks or feels as an individual — everybody always thinks and feels as a community and what emerges, the spirit of the time, in fact demands obedience. Nevertheless, one can say "no." Any major change has begun with a small "no" and there were already protests when the first slave ships set off, when the first Indios were worked to death. It takes a while for a small "no" to become a big one, public morality frequently lags behind political or economic developments, but eventually it gets to this point and the lawmakers penalize something that for a long time bothered very few people. Our consciousness never exactly reflects the external circumstances — human beings are too recalcitrant for this, and even the most powerful systems are too contradictory. Thank goodness we people are unpredictable and there are always some who resist the prevailing conditions. We were not born to run with the pack. Conformism is not a law of nature.

Nevertheless, there is still the question of what makes individuals rebel, how this gradual recognition process begins in the face of all opposition and finally leads to the abolition of slavery, the prohibition of torture, rebellion against something that has been taken for granted. My answer is that it is because people — in increasingly large numbers — empathize with the situation of the victim. For the victims were never in any doubt, for them slavery was always reprehensible, for them the invisible evil was always real and also highly visible. Only the rest of us were blind, as long we believed in the logic of the perpetrators, namely the logic of personal advantage. The utilitarian logic Satan had tried during the temptation of Jesus in the desert.

We have thus added another, again disturbing finding to our knowledge about evil. Good and evil are not self-evident. What this means with respect to the serpent's promise is that it's not easily fulfilled. The fruit of the tree of knowledge does not have an immediate effect. We're only able to distinguish between good and evil when we look at things from the perspective of the victim. The perspective of the one who is suffering. The one whose human dignity is denied in front of us. Whom we no longer consider as our equal.

Seeing things from the perspective of the victim . . . not too much to ask, one might think. But in fact it's a great deal to ask. Because we're actually reluctant to do so. We really don't want to change our perspective because that means identifying with the losers. And which of us can bring ourselves to do so, against the pressure of public opinion, the power of what appears to be a normal state of affairs, and our own need to be among the winners? Only people who are self-confident can do this. People who have achieved moral autonomy, great inner freedom, and independence. So initially there are many followers but few rebels. This is the autonomy Jesus talked about. The autonomy that comes with being oriented morally not to the existing conditions, but to what is timelessly valid.

Because our "no" needs a fixed reference point. A value, belief or authority that has established itself independently of the main, ever-changing spirit of the times. A fixed point, a starry heaven, a God. Without such a reference point, we are indeed in danger of becoming pure products of our respective conditions, copies of the outside world and blind to evil, which is concealed in the normal state of affairs.

Are we perhaps now well on our way to achieving this? Is it this that is clouding our visions of the future to the point of total hopelessness?

EViL

THE FALL

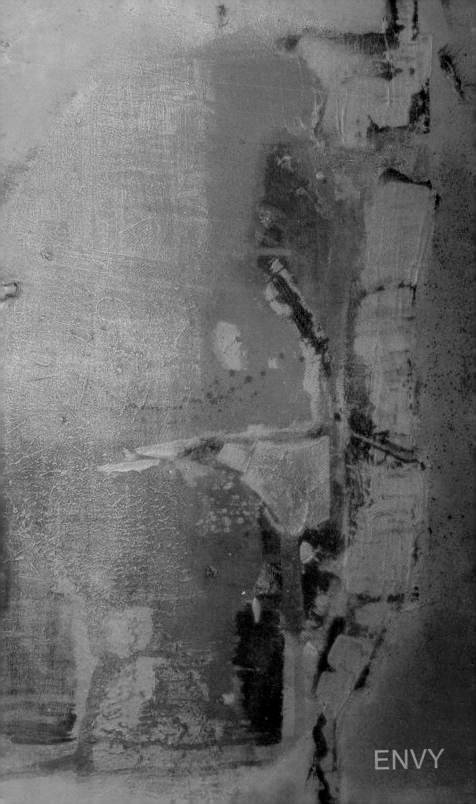

ENVY

GREED

NARCiSSiSM

HUBRiS

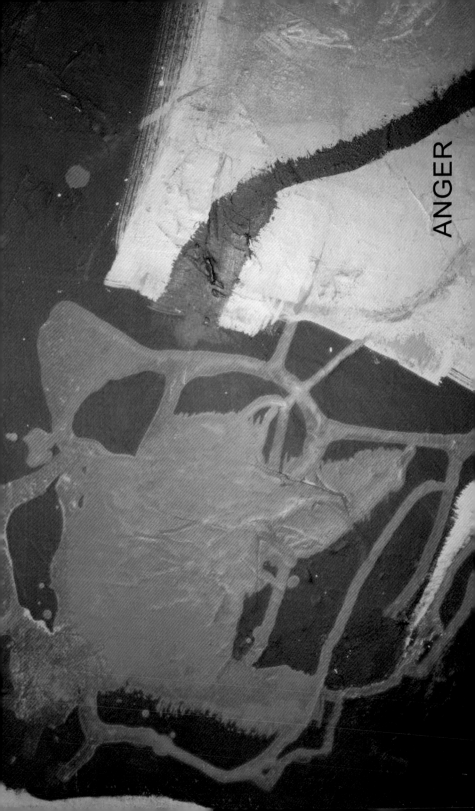

ANGER

FAiTHLESSNESS

11

Is human dignity inviolable?

But have we now come away empty-handed? Don't we have a wonderful instrument for identifying evil? A term that's ideal as a fixed reference point especially since it seems to be everlasting — at any rate it was used equally by ancient philosophers and Thomas Aquinas and other medieval theologians. I'm talking about human dignity. It has never gone out of fashion, and since the Enlightenment it has been even more popular. The first article of the German constitution also opens with the words "Human dignity shall be inviolable."

A sentence that couldn't be clearer. Don't we thus have a generally recognized formula that enables us to reliably distinguish between good and evil? In the political context, certainly, it's intended to prevent despotism on the part of the state, but a universal moral standard can be derived from it as well. You could, for example, say that evil is anything that violates human dignity.

And then you hesitate. At least that's how I react. Why, I wonder, doesn't it simply say "Human beings shall be inviolable?" And then immediately I have a second question. What does "inviolable" mean? Suddenly I find that the first article of our German constitution is an enigma. Isn't it then sufficient to simply speak of human beings here?

But let's first have a look at the term dignity. Its general meaning is well known: dignity puts human beings in a special light, gives them an importance that inspires respect. With respect to mankind as a whole, this implies that every individual deserves a respect due to no other living being. Only human beings are entitled to this. And this entitlement in turn arises from a quality that makes human beings unique and special. We're convinced of this anyway, but it's not inappropriate to put particular emphasis on human dignity — it defines us humans as creatures that owe something to one another. And to some extent as demanding beings who can't just be treated as anyone sees fit. To speak only of human beings would indeed not be going far enough.

But what exactly is meant by "inviolable"? Is this a statement of fact? Does it mean this dignity can never ever be taken away from human beings? That it represents an indestructible quality that's inherent in every person? In this case you have to imagine human dignity as a kind of protective cover, something that gives every individual an unassailable aura — or you could almost say confers holiness. Or is this "inviolable" meant as an admonition, an appeal? Does it call on us not to violate dignity because it is the most valuable but also the most sensitive part of man? What is then meant here is that certain circumstances or experience could cause damage, so that everyone's dignity should be handled with extreme care.

One thing is in any case evident: the first article of the constitution names something that absolutely has to be named when dealing with the relationship between human beings or between the state and the citizens. Something that identifies and distinguishes every person from the beginning and virtually defines his or her uniqueness, something for which respect can be claimed at any time. If dignity is the most profound characteristic of mankind, can it ever be endangered? Can it really be damaged or even destroyed by another person?

If the answer is yes, this means that in every encounter with another person our human dignity is at stake and that it must always be acknowledged and confirmed anew in our dealings with each other? It is as if we make a pact between each other every time with the following content: I acknowledge and respect in you the uniqueness we have in common. In this way we are equal and want to treat each other accordingly ... What we are then basically being required to do in order to preserve human dignity is to see ourselves in every other person! Consider him or her as our mirror image, as our equal, or in Christian terms, as our brother or sister.

Would everything be well then? Could evil be banned like this?

I'm afraid not. Because everything I might deny or take away from someone else represents a temptation, and equality always arouses feelings of competition. Doesn't even the blindest oppressor know that he is maltreating his equals? And isn't this precisely the perverse charm of his abominable rule? Mightn't it be the case that recognizing the other person as a brother doesn't necessarily result in friendly treatment but may be precisely the cause of maltreatment? Don't we know that from the family? What constellation of human relationships is more dynamic, more explosive? And this applies particularly to the relationship between brothers! How much jealousy, envy, and secret resentment can accumulate here! More than among friends and colleagues and definitely more than among strangers.

My equal? That can be positively understood as an invitation to strike out. There's too much similarity, too much we have common! Am I not unique? Must I put up with this threat to my uniqueness? Doesn't my self respect demand that I neutralize this other person, who's different in spite of all we have in common, who in truth doesn't want to be equal to me, who only apes me and at the same time ridicules me. In other words mustn't I thoroughly humiliate him until he's lost precisely that which makes him a human being and a competitor, namely his dignity?

Evil is therefore by no means banned if I see myself in the other person. You can even be scared of your own mirror image and want to smash it — this probably happens even more often than we realize, not only in concentration camps, in the Gulag and

Guantanamo. However, this then raises the question of whether oppressors achieve their goal? Do their plans succeed? Can human beings actually lose their dignity and still be human? They would then have lost their hallmark, their seal of approval, would become naked creatures and thus possibly ultimately unworthy of life ...

This is actually inconceivable. What it would mean is that evil would succeed in excluding individuals from the human community. I'd rather stick to the conviction that the humiliated, the ridiculous, and even those whose humanity is warped still retain their human dignity. Even an Adolf Hitler, even a Josef Stalin remains a human being under all circumstances — and they can no more be deprived of their human dignity than the concentration camp prisoner or the slave who's traded like merchandise. The dignity of man would then be indestructible, a quality that has always existed and can't be impaired — something that's possibly received, like a dowry. But if no one can be robbed of their special status within creation, what is then the reason for this obligation to respect human dignity, this first, supreme commandment of our constitution?

This question can best be answered if we use a common, generally accepted definition of human dignity. The definition that Immanuel Kant (1724–1804) supplied.

According to him, human dignity is an end in itself. What this means is that human beings don't need to either justify or explain their existence. We have a right to live and this right is not deducible, it's beyond all discussion, it's an unshakable, unquestionable basic fact. At most it might be asked how broadly life is being defined here. Is it only the life stripped to the bare essentials that's experienced by a maltreated, tortured prisoner in jail? Surely not. The same right also includes physical and emotional integrity, freedom, and much more. Human dignity then has many facets and many rights that can be derived from it and in practice, as everybody knows, these rights are indeed threatened by physical assault, deprivation of liberty or paternalism. The source of all these rights, however, would be the self-evidence of the human right to exist, so that what can be derived from the highest commandment of human dignity is that no one can ask others to justify their existence or substantiate their right to live. "Inviolable" is thus meant in two ways, as a statement and as a summons.

With human dignity an area of freedom is thus staked out. Also an area of security and self-confidence, because the associated rights never expire. As long as there is still life in a human being — and perhaps beyond — he or she is characterized by this dignity. It is our hallmark, the seal that confirms we are human beings. And nothing associated with human dignity has to be proved. However, it can't be proved either. And that's the problem.

It's doubtless reassuring to know that no one, no matter how powerful, can stand judge over my dignity. But what's the use of my claim to life and liberty if it ultimately can't be reasoned to exist? If the mind demands proof that can't be provided? Wouldn't my claim be exposed as a mere assertion and presumption? What can I then base this claim on, if I raise it? What's the authority behind this claim?

Such questions are pointless if we don't presume the existence of a supreme authority that has assigned human beings their exceptional position in the natural struggle for existence. Only religion is aware of these unquestionable and at the same time unprovable assumptions. Looked at in this way, human dignity is a quality from which practical claims can indeed be derived but in itself belongs to a dimension outside tangible reality. It stands and falls with the acceptance of a higher authority. It is inextricably linked with the belief in one God who by this means distinguishes man from the rest of creation. For the Christian, human dignity is founded in the fact that man is made in the image of God. This belief manifests itself incidentally even today, when we describe unimaginable atrocities as blasphemous.

With this, however, our hopes of finding a formula for evil have been dashed again. For while it's true that everything that violates human dignity can be classified as evil, evil doesn't always also violate human dignity, or get anywhere near this innermost, sacred human quality. Nevertheless human dignity provides us with a fixed reference point for establishing and preserving the rule of law.

But we have nevertheless found out something new about evil. If human dignity isn't our own invention, if we owe our special position within creation to God, then it's not enough to identify evil among ourselves. Then evil also affects our relationship to God.

But in any case, human dignity is a key to the infinitely vast space that opens up in us. For me it expresses the mystery of humankind, our unpredictability, self-will, incomprehensibility. This is what to me seems to constitute our dignity, that we don't fit any formula or calculation, can't be defined and so forever remain a mystery, an open variable. We thus have a share in a sphere beyond rationally ascertainable nature. We are to some extent part of another world.

12

The abolition of the past

A man and a young woman are sitting together in a restaurant, he's around sixty and she's in her mid-twenties. During their conversation, the man speaks about the attitude to life prevalent in his youth. "At your age we felt born to be winners," he says to her. "This optimism has waned over the years, but at that time we felt capable of literally anything. We were convinced we had a terrific life ahead of us." The young woman doesn't reply, but brings up the topic again at their next meeting. She says that this kind of self-assurance is foreign to her and she has never experienced it. That she was amazed to hear of it and when she asked her young friends, they could only shake their heads. None of them had had a similar experience. And no one wanted to believe that someone could have experienced such a phase of evidently unfounded euphoria . . .

The scene could have been taken from a movie or a novel. However, it was something that was described to me. Would it be too much to see it as symptomatic? Characteristic of the break which occurred at some point in the past two or three decades, the chasm separating the present generation's experience of the world from that of previous generations? I would go even further. I would speak of the end of an era. An era in which people repeatedly manifested an almost incomprehensible confidence, an almost foolhardy level of courage. Not because times were so good or life so easy, but because after every disappointment they discovered in themselves unsuspected strength and the ability to surpass themselves. Or to put it in the words of this vanished time: through faith they came close to God or through reason became more like God — or both. I would like to explain this at greater length.

We don't automatically understand ourselves as a race any more than we understand evil. We have no clear idea of ourselves, which is why the human image changes over time. And somehow the two things are connected, where we locate the source of evil and how we see ourselves, because one of the most worrying basic questions is always what do we have the courage to do in the struggle against evil, how strong are we and what are our limits? Depending on the answer, the image of man is sometimes more pessimistic and sometimes more optimistic but on one point people were long in agreement: man is an unfinished species, as Nietzsche said. With him this statement is of a pessimistic nature, but it is usually based on the confidence that we're far from having used up our emotional and mental potential and that we therefore mustn't be satisfied with our moral development and have a long way to go. This awareness animates our minds, galvanizes our forces, and inspires a Pico della Mirandola to appeal emphatically to us to use our enormous creative potential to constantly perfect ourselves — all in the awareness of an infinitely ambitious goal. The reference point of all efforts was called God.

Of course, there is also a danger in this. The desire to be like God can lead to arrogance and megalomania. But it can also produce the courage to aspire to high ideals and the willingness to make a huge effort to achieve them. You may also see in the belief in our potential for moral improvement a certain self-glorification, but I think it is a great asset to see oneself in this light — for me it is a reaction to the fact that since the Fall we've been living in a state of unexploited potential and therefore can expect a lot of ourselves. But in the background the image of God always remains as our ultimate and greatest model — albeit undoubtedly unattainable. It's virtually as if the human race has been set the task of finding the way back to God.

That's not even a particularly pious statement. These words even pass the lips of rationalists, of atheists. Thus the most famous existentialist writer, Jean-Paul Sartre (1905-80), notes laconically: "Man wants to be like God. This is his fate." Of course the question of how to achieve this goal, whether through faith, willpower or assertiveness, remains unanswered. But in any case, in their unfinished state human beings see the opportunity to develop immeasurably; because nothing is programmed, therefore nothing is impossible, everything is open and they're therefore entitled to have great hopes. In other words, the awareness of our incompleteness gives rise to an uplifting feeling of inner freedom. This was probably what the man in the restaurant experienced in his youth. This experience was probably what the young woman and her friends were no longer familiar with.

What has changed? One thing in particular, I would say: in the silent revolution of the last few decades, not only has God been abolished, but evil too has gradually been taken out of circulation. And all at once we no longer see any need to improve morally. We've become reconciled to being as we always were, basically harmless, loving and nice — in other words a finished species. It's therefore pointless to intervene in the lives of others and burden them with moral standards — what truth or authority is this going to be based on? A surprising change given that the mystery of man was a source of perplexity for such a long time, but none the less consistent for all that. Because if our only point of reference is ourselves, we have no reason to doubt ourselves. All that we can now actually establish is that I am what I am and from this conclude that we human beings are innocent, let us do as we want.

Where does this take us now? It's impossible to say with certainty, but it's evident that the rudder has swung right round. The current determination to surpass oneself is based at any rate on an insight never granted to previous generations: human beings can be reinvented. Like everything else in the world they can be measured and decrypted and resolved into data and thus be so perfectly adapted to the circumstances that they are no longer disruptive.

Had people simply been looking so far in the wrong place on the assumption that the weak point lay in one's soul, will, or consciousness and this was where it had to be tackled? But perhaps that was not so wrong either, perhaps the approach should just have been much more radical. Nevertheless attempts were made. Where the great ideologies of the last century held sway, there had already been moves to abolish the soul, to eliminate the will, and to switch off consciousness. That was a beginning. But what was not done — and admittedly the means were lacking — was to intervene in the biological nature of the human race and change it fundamentally. That is now possible. The remarkable finding of the present is that man is programmable and we have the necessary technical means to hand.

Meanwhile people and technology have come closer together. So close that they already form a unit. The smartphone has become part of the body like the pacemaker, and without a computer we would be helpless. But it's also now that we really are moving in the direction of fantastic artificial paradises. A complete fusion of man and technology is foreseeable, and in the opinion of the philosopher Stefan Lorenz Sorgner we can expect nothing but good from this — life will become more livable and man not only happier but also morally better.

Who we are, what we can do and what we experience will hardly matter in the future because brain pacemakers will keep us in a good mood and spare us mental suffering. Brain implants will help us to achieve fantastic intellectual feats, facilitate the learning of foreign languages, and improve our memory. In our technically optimized form we will function in an unprecedented way and even our destiny will be foreseeable and predictable. With *in vitro* fertilization, says Sorgner, only those children will be selected who have the greatest chance of a good life — so no defects or malformations, no losers. However, the Jewish–Christian image of man will have to be sacrificed. Human beings will no longer be able to claim to be the crown of creation because there will only be marginal genetic differences between man and the animals. In purely biological terms, therefore, there is nothing to be said against abandoning all scruples. We'll then have ourselves entirely at our own disposal. Released from all moral liabilities, we'll be able to act freely. We'll all be able to choose what improvements we want to make to ourselves, we'll all be allowed to develop in whatever direction we want and of course even good and evil will be at the discretion of the individual — a personal matter, a matter of taste. Meanwhile building a replica of the human brain and eternal life are already on the agenda in the Google laboratory.

Sorgner no longer speaks of human beings, but of post-humans. What this means exactly we can learn from the American moviemaker and video artist Ryan Trecartin, whose entire work is about the effects of the digital revolution.

The people of the future, we are told, will primarily make use of their right to self-exposure. As actors of their own lives they will stop at nothing that could cause a sensation in the world of the digital media. "Everything will be recorded," says Trecartin "Talent shows and wiretapping programs will only have been a prelude. Warm-up exercises for a world in which all living beings are recorded to the point of being coded and will be reproducible and changeable at will." Nothing will remain of the world we know. With Trecartin this perishes in a firework of images and noises emitted by new bizarre creatures, figures that constantly change their name and gender, act and speak incoherently, and make self-confessions that are meaningless because the self no longer exists. Under pressure to put themselves most effectively on show, their identity and character have fallen by the wayside so that these post-humans reel in a mindless dance towards self-dissolution.

As you can see, even outrageous scenarios have now become readily conceivable and have their advocates, defenders, and prophets. And suddenly you see the playful, peaceful, and serene demigods dreamed of by Heinrich Heine and the superman envisaged by Nietzsche as the only way out of human misery in a different light. They were no figments of the imagination. They are actually appearing on the horizon — prosthetic gods deprived of any individuality, all occupied with themselves and at the same time desperately concentrating on the effect they're making.

A realistic vision? Certainly. The future has already begun and the visionaries are only thinking further along the lines of what is already emerging. The primal impulse to experiment has prevailed and taken over everything. We can confidently believe that these nightmare paradises are feasible. Another aspect of this occurs to me. It looks to me as if the human race has thus taken flight. Flight from itself. As if the fusion of man and machine, the dissolution of individuality was the only way out of an otherwise hopeless situation. In any case, it implies an escape from responsibility when we act according to the principle that the machine is innocent, so let it do what it wants. Is our situation really so chaotic?

I believe that in the last decades of the 20th century a decision of immense consequence was made. It has affected the whole Western world and is of a fundamental nature, but of course it has only gradually taken effect, manifesting itself as a cultural upheaval stretching over decades, and it's only now possible to start assessing its importance as its consequences start appearing. It's the decision to see the present as the beginning of the future. This may not initially sound so outrageous. But when you consider that previously the present had always been seen as the extension of the past, you see what a change of attitude this represents. If today is no longer the last day of the past but the first day of the future, we have rotated our relationship to time by 180 degrees and must completely change how we think and feel. This is what has happened. Ordered by no one but wanted by many. Which is how silent revolutions always come about.

Because it's entirely different whether I live in the awareness that the past has never stopped, or under the impression that the future has already begun. I either see myself at the end of a development or at the beginning of a new age. I either feel like a student or administrator of an inheritance, or like a creator and originator with the power to do whatever I want. In the second case, I not only have the right but also the duty to wipe out consciousness of the past. The great revolutions in France and Russia as well as the Cultural Revolution in China tried to do this with brute force, but without overwhelming success. This time renunciation of the past has succeeded without the guillotine, show trials and mass executions. How was this possible?

Our history is full of bitter lessons. It has a store of disappointments. We have seen in the historical chapters how pessimistic those who grasped the situation repeatedly felt; people were already on the verge of despair due to the continual setbacks in the battle against evil. With the wars and exterminations of the 20th century, this history reached its gruesome climax. Apart from the unbearable guilt, what are the lessons to be learned from the piles of corpses in the concentration camps and the orgies of destruction of two world wars? Didn't everything point to a complete failure of our civilization? Was it worth continuing at all?

Who can write poetry any more in the face of such sheer horror, as it was said in Germany in the postwar period. The shock over the inconceivable happenings was expressed in full in the 1960s and 1970s and all at once the entire history of Europe seemed to be infected with the virus of evil. The writer Karlheinz Deschner wrote a ten-volume crime story of Christianity, in which he portrayed the whole history of the Church history as a series of transgressions, but basically one now saw one's own past in general in the light of a crime story, a domain of evil which one no longer wanted to have anything to do with. This suspicion of one's own culture and history mainly affected Germany, but it also affected the rest of the Western world. People looked back and found traces of an unbearable guilt everywhere in the past.

Perhaps it's unavoidable under these circumstances to demolish the bridges to this past in order to carry on, and carry on we must. But there is one thing we should remember. The decision to no longer see today as the endpoint of the past but as the starting point of the future is possibly the most radical decision ever made. A panic reaction, only to be understood as a dramatic rescue attempt, a desperate liberation operation comparable with that of a captivated rat gnawing through its own leg to escape from a trap. For up until then culture had been the memory of mankind. Historical knowledge preserved not only facts, but the history of the long and painful experience that preceded every insight. It also allowed us to understand the present as a stage of development, as the result of countless successful and unsuccessful attempts, from which we could at least conclude for our own lives that the present must always be treated with caution and man is always hanging by a thread ...

The fact is that we've disconnected ourselves from the history of our origins. As an older person you'll occasionally come across this circumstance through an unbiased, I might almost say ingenuous remark by a young person: "World War Two? That was long before my time, it doesn't interest me," as somebody recently said to me. What a bizarre logic I think, and then I remember that this person belongs to a generation for whom only the future counts. He's virtually looking into a promising void and after all that has happened, what presents itself to him has an extremely beneficial effect. For the future requires nothing from us, we merely have to let it happen. It doesn't teach us any lessons, it doesn't pose any moral questions, there's no guilt involved, it releases us from every responsibility, it's a non-binding nothing. Above all it allows us to believe that salvation is within reach and feasible through our own willpower, so that everyone's assured of the greatest freedom, because we owe nothing to anyone but ourselves.

The renunciation of the past has rendered many things unnecessary. In the sanctuary of the future there's a mighty altar on which what was previously valid is constantly being sacrificed. And the priests of this sanctuary accept everything without examining the value of the things they burn. They don't even require proof that something has had its day, as long as "obsolete" is written on it. Since this sacrificial fire has been burning, it seems that just about every social change has a chance of success. Reality itself has become purely conditional, as the visions of the future summarized in this chapter verify. And anyone who lodges an objection against modernization is exposed significantly as a "reactionary" or even worse as "someone living in the past."

Because what's being burned is merely the impositions of the past — impositions such as the Doctrine of the Mean, beliefs and principles, standards and certainties. Precisely that which is no longer compatible with the freedom given us by the future. We are therefore doomed — to the delight of some and the dismay of others — to get by without any binding rules about basic ethical questions, whether pertaining to education, family, reproduction, sexuality or to the whole direction of our lives, in other words questions of sense and nonsense, worth and worthlessness. One thing has in the meantime become as good as another, right and wrong can no longer be distinguished, the dividing line between good and evil is blurred. Everything that served as moral orientation or a guideline in the past has been dealt with and everything that was once valid can change within a short time into its opposite — it's best to stay out of it and not even form an opinion. But where there are no more ethical limits, in case of doubt everything becomes a matter of audacity, and the deciding factor concerning good and evil, right and wrong is success.

We feel comfortable with this ethical fatalism. But no sparks can be struck from this spongy material, no sparks of joy or hope that especially in the early years of adult life can fire an apparently unfounded enthusiasm. The mystification of the young woman in the restaurant could mainly have been caused by the fact that the rampant indifference to fundamental life questions no longer releases spirited energies. It reduces basic emotional tension to the extent that only lukewarm consent with all manner of opinions and fashions is left.

Moreover the experiences of the last decades make it abundantly clear that we can't solve the problem of evil by closing our eyes. As Adam and Eve found themselves in the real world after their experiment and had to bear the consequences, we too will not be able to rise above reality. And the reality is that you don't throw your own history overboard unpunished.

13

All you can eat

I was to give an interview. As usual, a few things had to be clarified in advance by phone and finally the lady asked me a question that interested her personally. I earned money with my books and lectures, didn't I, what did I do with it?

Evidently she remembered something about a vow of poverty. "The money goes into the renovation of Sant'Anselmo and fellowships for students from poor countries," I replied. "Well, don't you feel any need to keep something for yourself?" she then asked in a disbelieving tone. I explained to her that I wouldn't even know what to do with any money I put aside for myself... She said goodbye rather irritably. I was very likely somewhat suspect in her eyes. She probably thought hankering after money and possessions was a law of nature. In my experience most people believe that.

Is it a law of nature?

In 2007 Matthew Taylor, a former top manager of the American investment bank Goldman Sachs, was put in jail for nine months for not disclosing a position in futures contracts amounting to billions. The New York court stated in its judgment that Taylor had amassed a total of 8.3 billion dollars from bets on futures and had concealed this from his employer by making a false report. The 34-year old stockbroker also had to pay a fine equivalent to the losses he had inflicted on Goldman Sachs with his risky transactions, which amounted to 18 million dollars.

We recall that this was the time of the first bank scandals and crashes. We ordinary people had previously had no idea that behind the scenes the banks, stock exchanges, and investment companies, in other words the entire financial world, was a madhouse. We then had to get used to unimaginable sums that seemingly came out of nothing and went back to nothing and to our horror find that there was not just *one* Matthew Taylor but hundreds and thousands of his ilk. We were quite dumbfounded to discover a new type of human being: the 25-year-old who comes within an inch of causing a global catastrophe with crazy money transactions and yet can still sleep at night. And suddenly we look into an abyss of — what? Irresponsibility, greed, hubris? Aren't these words far too weak? It was certainly staggering.

Or did these processes also obey a natural law? In other words: had it always been like this?

A brief look at the past at any rate teaches us that we've always been greedy. This can readily be inferred from the Old Testament. For example, the patriarchs Abraham, Isaac, and Jacob had amassed considerable wealth as cattle breeders. They didn't come by this wealth easily, and Jacob at least acquired his in a dubious way, namely by fraud. There was nothing wrong with wealth, in fact it was seen as a sign of divine blessing. Of course it wasn't generated like it is on the New York stock exchange. Camels and cattle can't be pulled out of a hat, so that wealth couldn't assume absurd dimensions. It wasn't possible to make quick money, and those who were nevertheless successful were looked up to by others and could feel blessed. Harsh words about greed and avarice are thus scarcely to be found in the Old Testament, which at most criticizes the predatory practices of the powerful.

But in the book of Qoheleth (or Ecclesiastes), so already in the 3rd century BC, we find a number of critical reflections on the topic of money. In a down-to-earth tone, the author tackles the topic from a psychological perspective and gets so precisely to the heart of the matter that it's worth quoting a few sentences. "The lover of money will not be satisfied with money; nor the lover of wealth, with gain. This also is vanity. Sweet is the sleep of laborers, whether they eat little or much; but the surfeit of the rich will not let them sleep. As they came from their mother's womb, so they shall go again, naked as they came; they shall take nothing for their toil . . . All human toil is for the mouth, yet the appetite is not satisfied."

A superb text. There is little more to add. Does money make you insatiable? Does greed increase with the degree of wealth? Even 2,000 years later the French Enlightenment philosopher Montesquieu wondered why money didn't come under the law of scarcity, because the less you have of something, the more you appreciate it. What is even more amazing is that people can't and won't spend all their money; if the wealthy nevertheless continue to increase their assets they must either think they're immortal or else money-making has become a way of life devoid of any meaningful purpose. And then anxiety about money gives the rich no peace. This makes me think of Uli Hoeness, who looked at his mobile every few minutes to check on the current state of his shares, a gambler who didn't seem to believe in his luck. As soon as he put his phone down he felt withdrawal symptoms like a drug addict and Hoeness himself compared his harassed, restless state of mind to that of an addict. And finally, wealth doesn't deliver what people expect of it "yet the appetite is not satisfied." The rich man is willing to take a lot of effort and aggravation on board for something that isn't enough to make him happy because his mind and soul are undersupplied. All in all a rather pessimistic summary of the situation. With the same dry realism, the writer of Qoheleth however shortly afterwards pays tribute to the pleasures of wealth when he writes "Feasts are made for laughter; wine gladdens life, and money meets every need . . ." This means that without money you would probably have less fun — this shouldn't be forgotten either.

The New Testament is more abrasive on the subject. In the

meantime, people had had more experience of exploitation and ruthless enrichment tactics and the power of money was seen in a much more critical light. Jesus himself had a clear opinion on this — but was not against the rich or wealth itself. His warnings were about greed, precisely because of its addictive nature, because it takes away our freedom to decide and enslaves the soul. This is the context in which his famous saying on the subject of money and ownership should be understood: "It is easier for a camel to go through the eye of a needle than for someone who is rich to enter the kingdom of God." If I understand this sentence correctly, Jesus isn't condemning wealth, but sees the blind greed with which the rich cling to their possessions as the biggest obstacle to achieving inner freedom. In other words, those who put all their mental and spiritual energies into material things lose sight of their life goal and their sensibility is dulled.

The early Christians thus rejected wealth as the purpose or meaning of life. "But those who want to be rich fall into temptation … and many senseless and harmful desires that plunge people into ruin and destruction," says the author of the first letter to Timothy and describes the ideal of Christian modesty as follows: "But if we have food and clothing we will be content with these." The Christian attitude is put in a nutshell in another sentence of this letter: "For the love of money is a root of all kinds of evil." And this was the standard approach for a long time — at least in theory.

After all, it was possible to take a stand against it. You could reject greed and the striving for possessions altogether. Benedict, founder of the Benedictine order, was one of those who did so, likewise all the orders of monks, and freely choosing to live a life of poverty was even attractive to many people. We mustn't forget this because nowadays it sounds unbelievable and of course it has always been the exception. But I don't want to write a history of greed here, it would fill libraries and I'll also come back to it again later. However, before we return to the present I would like to cite an example of the strangest characteristic of greed: the fact that it regularly afflicts precisely those who have enough or more than enough.

In the 16th century, Antwerp became a wealthy trading metropolis and if the painters and poets at that time are to be believed, greed and avarice spread like the plague through the Flemish port. In any case it was unknown on this scale and the dismay it produced has left its traces in numerous inscriptions and paintings. Beneath a copper engraving of 1558 showing two cloth merchants in dispute one can read the following comment: "There's no one who doesn't seek his own advantage everywhere. No one who doesn't seek himself in everything he does . . . Everyone is greedy." And on a painting from the beginning of the same century you see two usurers (today one would say "bankers") whose physiognomies are distorted with expressions of grim satisfaction and greed. The faces of the two are pinched and closed like tied money bags and their expression says we're no longer accessible, we've withdrawn into a world in which nothing's of importance except the pile of money in front of us . . . The painter Quentin Massays was certain of finding an audience that shared his disdain for such unpleasant contemporaries.

Greed — a law of nature? This much at least can be concluded from this brief retrospective: paradoxically it goes hand-in-hand with wealth. By no means everyone is insatiable, only the sated appear to be insatiable. As absurd as it sounds — it confirms the age-old observation that money makes us addicted, dependent and unfree. No, not money as such, but money in large amounts. Although never before in human history have we thought in such astronomical sums as we do now.

"I'm grateful for the opportunity to speak in public for the first time about my crimes." With these words, the American stockbroker Bernie Madoff began his explanation at the end of his trial in court. "While I was pursuing my fraudulent activities it was clear to me that I was doing wrong or rather acting criminally . . . I'm here today to take responsibility for this crime by pleading guilty."

Madoff then went on to explain in detail how up until the year 2008 he'd succeeded in cheating about 4,800 individuals, charities, companies, and hedge funds of a total of 65 billion dollars: instead of investing the money of his customers as promised in the shares and options of major companies he paid it into a bank account. If someone wanted their winnings paid out or their investments back he simply withdrew the sum from this account, which was constantly being swelled with new money. He wanted to stop in the first year, Madoff explained to the court, but only got deeper in. At the end his maneuvers amounted to the biggest fraud case in history. In 2009 he was given a 150-year jail sentence.

65 billion dollars! Amassed and squandered by a single person. Evidently there was no barrier he couldn't surmount. Anybody who made financial transactions, not just in America, seemed to act according to the motto *après moi le déluge*. Apparently we had — and still have — the most irrational economic and financial system of all time. And this Bernie Madoff was not even an unscrupulous gangster. Madoff had made his name as a generous philanthropist and was a highly respected member of the upper echelons of society. Was it still at all possible to make individuals responsible for this disaster? Wasn't the whole system rotten? Was there a different explanation for the collective moral failure? Given the immense damage, you could probably say that with this whole affair of banks and stock markets evil had asserted itself to an unbelievable degree.

And I find a second aspect of the bank scandal no less worrisome. I'm talking about the fact that many people, Americans and Europeans alike, are fascinated by these fraudsters and their crimes.

In his movie *The Wolf of the Wall Street*, the director Martin Scorsese traces the criminal career of Jordan Belfort. In a frenzy of greed, egocentrism, narcissism, and unscrupulousness, this Belfort had cheated thousands of guileless people out of their money with worthless securities and become fantastically rich in the process, but was finally convicted and imprisoned. In the last scenes of the movie Belfort is seen appearing in front of a large audience. These people have come because they want to find out what his "secret of success" is and they hang spellbound on the lips of the grand master of fraud as he introduces them to the art of cheating. For them Belfort is apparently a hero, a cult figure. This final sequence could be interpreted as a sarcastic comment of the director on the cultural climate in which people like Belfort can rise to become stars. But it's not an invention. It corresponds to reality. Since his release from prison, Belfort has actually been giving seminars on fraud and people are actually flocking to hear him. Evidently everyone wants to become like him, as self-centered, greedy, narcissistic, and unscrupulous — and as successful. They are all dreaming of a career in crime — this is the only explanation I can find for it.

And this really is something new. Things have clearly changed quite a lot after all since Adam and Eve. If the main goal in life is to make a lot of money, if greed has become a normal part of humankind's make-up, then it can't be explained any more in terms of a law of nature. Then something has gone fundamentally wrong with us.

However, it all began in a small way. In postwar Germany, for example, with a harmless, plausible slogan. Prosperity for all been promised by the Minister of Economic Affairs Ludwig Erhard, who thus formulated an initial, high-priority goal which in principle was valid for all the countries of Western Europe that were economically weakened at the end of the war. For the sake of simplicity, I'll confine myself here to Germany, but the development I want to describe took place in exactly the same way in other parts of the Western world. It represents the practical, everyday side of what I called in the last chapter the abolition of the past, the decision in favor of the future, and virtually leads us straight to the edge of the abyss into which we just have looked.

The beginning was still a matter of sheer necessity: it was

essential to start reconstructing the ruined country and people plunged into work, but also wanted to be rewarded for their efforts, they wanted to buy things, consume, participate in progress, and finally enjoy the fruits of their labor without having to regret it afterwards. The world of economics and consumerism was ideal for this, because it's neutral. It is untainted. It sets no conditions, raises no moral questions, is beyond good and evil and thus one can be lulled into thinking that producing and consuming is no sin. So here, after the disaster of the past, an area of activity presented itself that was above suspicion.

At some point this reconstruction period should have come to an end. At some point there should have been a return to more meaningful activities. Ludwig Erhard realized the moment had come in 1957. The worst was over and now it would have been possible to think about real life. However, as we've seen, greed increases with prosperity, and the future to which people now turned promised even greater prosperity. The magic words were progress and growth; what more did one need? People had unexpectedly found themselves in a world of wishes, which compared with the old world had the advantage of the wishes actually coming true — so why not stay with it? Now a name had to be found for an inhabitant of this new world. A term that expressed the nature of this being. And so the consumer was born. We became consumers.

Shouldn't we have woken up at least then? How could we have acquiesced to this? Consuming means eating or using up; the designation consumer reduces us to the animal activities of feeding and devouring or in plain terms to voracity. It implies that the main characteristic of man is assimilation, as if the only purpose of our lives was to purchase and wear out various products. Actually the word consumer should long ago have been declared taboo. But it hasn't been. It's prevailed and become the generic name of modern man. And I fear we've deserved this label. We've become consumers. In any case, we've largely behaved since then as consumers. And what I find even more alarming is that it seems the majority of us are willing to remain consumers. This has ushered in the next phase of the development which began with the harmless motto "Prosperity for all."

At social gatherings, comments like the following can be heard with increasing frequency: "Why do we still have theater? What do we still have opera houses for? Why not stop wasting money like this?" The speakers then justify this by saying, "Anyway, hardly anyone still goes. We can't afford this luxury for a shrinking minority. It's simply no longer cost-effective."

Such sentences often meet with approving nods. Everyone agrees that theater, opera houses, and similar institutions are economically pointless because they're unproductive. They're not worthwhile. They don't noticeably benefit society in financial terms. The utility of something must be reflected in tangible, visible, preferably material benefits; otherwise it's superfluous ... People have never taken things this far before: subjecting intellectual things to an accounting process where they show up as a loss. For the consumer, culture has become negligible. It doesn't present as a success story in which the above-mentioned tangible, measurable, and preferably pecuniary advantages have been produced. And this thinking is not only widespread, in the meantime it has taken over all areas of life. Disarmed by our moral and intellectual memory loss, we've surrendered ourselves entirely to the economic logic, according to which what is good is what pays and what is evil is what can only be put on the invisible account of our intellectual and spiritual maturity. With this we have granted the economy enormous power. The power to shape us in its image.

Because the economy has already presented us consumers with its own invoice. It expects us to submit ourselves to its requirements and play according to its rules if we want it to fulfill our wishes. Formerly this would have meant longer working hours or less pay. Today it means accepting a world and human image shaped in terms of the economy. It means identifying ourselves with its goals and believing in its promises.

To explain the hold the economy has on our thinking, let's look at the word efficiency. Originally efficiency meant the welcome characteristic of measures or machines to produce their desired effect. Meanwhile the same is expected of people. They have to transform themselves into career- and success-oriented bundles of activity, and they in turn see the world solely through the lens of efficiency. It goes without saying that they sacrifice themselves for the interests of the company — being a winner has its price — but everything else must work as perfectly as they do, from the coffee machine to their circle of friends.

They don't get hung up on questions to which there is no unambiguous answer. On an imaginary points system, they note which encounters have been fruitful, which tasks have been worthwhile, and how they themselves have performed. Their whole life is weighed up in this way and what can't be expressed in facts and figures isn't worthy of their attention. In this controlled existence, planning plays a prominent role. The life plan, organizing the necessary steps to success, working out how to present themselves, shaping their image. Everything must be right. Efficient people don't like surprises, certainly don't rely on their luck and must and want to become managers of themselves. Ultimately they are nothing more than well-oiled cogs in the gearbox of the economic universe.

When is everything perfect? When nothing impedes my progress. For decades, this thinking has been seeping into our consciousness and impregnating it against the temptation to search for happiness in life elsewhere other than in economic success. And since people can't be put onto the career track fast enough, kindergarten, school, training, and studies are also being made more and more efficient. And if you ask how human qualities such as understanding, compassion or even conscience can be developed under these circumstances, you are reassured that this too has been taken care of: people can catch up on this through coaching at any time. Social skills are now taught in seminars. Because for everything there are ready-made formulas and rudimentary social behavior can be taught as a technique, can be trained . . .

With this we've outgrown the consumer phase. Consumers still to some extent let themselves be served, efficiency-oriented people serve themselves. Now we're only one step away from the third phase, where the people pulling the levers of economic power have such an incredibly exaggerated opinion of themselves that they totally lose control of themselves and their actions, as happened in the so-called bank crisis. All we are now lacking is the appropriate human image that will license us to go mad.

In his book *Ego: Das Spiel des Lebens*, journalist Frank Schirrmacher describes how in recent decades a "new social monster" has been able to develop, created through the combined efforts of the military, economists, scientists, and the stockbrokers on Wall Street.

The starting point was the American military's search for a universal formula for human behavior in order to predict the actions of an opponent. Everything the researchers found pointed to the fact that all human activity is based on self-interest. Egoism is the formula that was found. Egoism is what primarily motivates everyone and that's all we need to know about it. Because there's nothing that can be done. Culture and education, morals and character pale before the power of human self-interest. It isn't therefore a matter of individuals. What we have here is a race that is simply put together, whose members all function in the same way according to a basic stimulus–response pattern, just like animals. Two things can be relied on: their fear of losing something and their greed for more.

This was interesting not only for the military but above all for the economy, particularly for the advertising business and the financial world. Because the formula worked. Those who applied it were superior to their competitors, but were particularly successful when it came to manipulating people. You couldn't go wrong when you assessed your counterpart according to this formula. Nor could you go wrong if you applied this formula to yourself and acted only in your own interest.

And thus the third phase begins.

For this cynical image of man was planted in the mind by a flood of self-help books, taught in universities, converted into corporate ideologies, and elevated to become the basic law of the market. It of course became the model for the Matthew Taylors, Bernie Madoffs, and Jordan Belforts juggling with billion dollars or euros. Thus people who were totally uninhibited sat at their computers amidst the flood of data from the stock markets and financial institutions — unfettered players in an unfettered financial world. Under such circumstances it would be absurd to ask about responsibility. The absolute egoist is as innocent as a poker player who defeats his opponent because he's better at bluffing. But who or what is then to blame?

It probably amounts to the fact that we've taken a wrong turning. As I said previously, the future is a non-binding nothing and whoever relies on it will be undermined. This is precisely what the visions of the future in the last chapter show: in the world of the self-optimizer and self-promoter pure egoism reigns. This world is populated by people without fellow human-beings, by beings without individuality, all underway in an empty universe on their own planets. Must we follow this path right to the end? In any case, we're in a dilemma. It was the London mayor Boris Johnson who spoke plainly about this dilemma at the end of 2013. Let's not fool ourselves, was his message — envy, greed, and egoism are the basis of our economic system. They are the indispensable driving forces of capitalism. But — he reassured his audience — this capitalism has the wonderful ability to change base motives into prosperity . . .

Must we thus resign ourselves to fact that we're heading for the next catastrophe? If we want to remain as consumers, if prosperity is still to be valued above everything else, then yes. In that case, I fear, we'll be pushed in droves into the giant mouth of the economy and enter like sleepwalkers, just like the representatives of society, led by a bishop or pope, who wander into the wide-open jaws of hell in medieval paintings. Because in that case it won't be possible to remedy the actual construction fault in our economic system: that it rewards the worst character flaws. This system turns what would formerly have been seen as vices, as the failure of every rational or moral instance, into virtues and personal advantage. It devalues the established values, it promotes and rewards the vices named by Boris Johnson, and if we look carefully we'll see that our economic system is now built on what were previously called deadly sins. This is what it capitalizes on and without them it wouldn't work.

We have thus gained a new insight into evil. We can assume that if the deadly sins have such an important effect on the economy, they won't be without effect in other areas of life. Meanwhile, of course, one should clarify first whether the deadly sins make sense to us at all today? Is such an antiquated term applicable in our day?

14

The deadly sins

The deadly sins undeniably stem from another time. A time when the fate of man wasn't attributed to the genes or external circumstances. They originate from a past in which man still had to answer for what he did and the struggle between good and evil was a major drama in the hidden, incomprehensible, and mysterious inner world that represented the most essential part of a person. And while they're old fashioned, they aren't sins.

This is actually a pity. Even those who consider the deadly sins to be the epitome of pathological religious morality will concede that this term exerts a grim fascination. It is associated with wickedness and eternal damnation and provides an inexhaustible stock of ideas that painters and writers in particular have drawn on down the ages for their human comedies and tragedies. But as uncannily attractive as this term may be, it conjures up totally false associations. It implies neither death nor sin. The deadly sins are actually mental aberrations — personality disorders we would say today — and were never intended to be used as a threat. They should rather be understood as an early warning system with which destructive or self-destructive tendencies could be identified before a person became completely unbalanced. And their history is worth relating.

For this we have to go back to the 4th century AD. In this period the desert monks in Egypt and Syria were attracting many followers. These monks lived in isolation in tiny cells far away from civilization, following strict ascetic rules, and what motivated them was the hope of being able to focus entirely on God in their solitude, undisturbed by the temptations of a society infected with greed, envy, and vanity. As became apparent, it wasn't easy. Many found out that it wasn't enough to sever all ties with civilization — even, and especially, in solitude they were vulnerable to the temptations of their previous lives. Apparently human beings have built-in urges that are determined to gain the upper hand, and in their perplexity these monks turned to a certain Evagrius Ponticus. Above all they wanted to know what symptoms would enable them to recognize in time that they were deviating from the path of liberation and self-control.

This Evagrius Ponticus (AD 346-99) was as it were the grey eminence of the desert monks, erudite, and an excellent psychologist. At the request of the monks, he compiled a list of eight natural impulses or driving forces that can become obsessions and thus lead to loss of self-control. His list is not a register of sins, he wasn't interested in individual, even inexcusable misdemeanors, he wanted to get to the bottom of what was bothering these monks. But even the driving forces he identified as causes are not in themselves evil, for the very reason that they arise involuntarily, apparently out of nowhere — nobody was immune to spontaneous feelings of pride, envy or jealousy, said Evagrius. What makes them dangerous is that over time they take root in the soul as vices if one gives in to them. I will illustrate his basic idea with an example.

One item on his list is gluttony and it's clear that he wasn't trying to spoil our enjoyment of a good meal, as is popularly believed. This is about excess. Uncontrolled eating behavior comes under the category of greed and thus fulfills the conditions of immoderation. If Evagrius had been familiar with the present conditions, if he had already known about the diet mania, he would probably have paired gluttony with anorexia, because permanent, compulsive self-control represents a lack of restraint similar to voracity. A psychologist would probably speak about infantile emotions, because both behavioral patterns demonstrate that the people concerned haven't yet learned to make decisions, to restrict themselves or moderate their behavior in one or the other direction. And the other items on his list are to be interpreted in the same way, namely as a warning against immoderation: lust, greed, anger, sorrow (in the sense of frustration), sloth (in the sense of depression), vainglory, and pride. Evagrius Ponticus did something very clever: he straightened out the considerable disorder in people's minds, gave names to the individual driving forces, and pointed out the related dangers. He thus gave his monks a method of psychological self-diagnosis, convinced that they could curb their desires through self-observation and willpower before any of these became an obsession. It was as it were an early form of psychoanalysis. His list is in any case the original version of the catalogue of deadly sins, although Evagrius never uttered the words "deadly sin", nor did Pope Gregory the Great (AD 540–604), who adopted the list later on, because it was generally useful for diagnosing spiritual aberrations.

Gregory made only two small changes: He put pride, which ranked last with Evagrius, at the top of the list — for him arrogance, the human tendency to megalomania, was the root of all evil. And then he reduced the number of main vices to the mystically charged figure of seven by deleting sorrow. The ambiguous term "deadly sins" took root in the 12th century, to some extent for reasons of clarity, on the grounds that the more drastic something is, the more easily it's remembered. There was still no thought of everlasting damnation — death here refers to the blunting, desolation, and gradual death of the soul that is dominated by one of these obsessions. In this state, however, human beings inevitably cause damage. They become sinners.

The deadly sins have thus always been a checklist for critical mental states, for symptoms of personality disorders. They didn't necessarily go hand in hand with moral condemnation of the person concerned. The deadly sins were an accurate and timelessly valid means of identifying the impulses that could damage individuals mentally to the point where they actually became a danger to themselves and others — this was their value.

Nevertheless they might have been displaced by the more differentiated instrument of modern psychology if they hadn't triumphantly reminded us of themselves in our time. It's hard to believe, but in a world dedicated to permanent growth that operates on the principle of immoderation, the list of immoderate forms of behavior drawn up by an ancient desert monk is more relevant than ever. And this world thinks nothing of openly committing itself to the deadly sins. It flirts, it even adorns herself with them when companies for example declare avarice to be sexy or sell their perfumes under names such as "Arrogance" or "Egoiste." Why not? The major vices of old have become the virtues of today, the indispensable foundation of our economic system. We're thus no longer talking about the false paths trodden by the individual. We're talking about the deadly sins as the way of life of an entire society. And perhaps this way of life is so attractive because once unleashed, the deadly sins have a thrilling effect generated by the releasing of the original forces and drives.

Let us look at the larger context. Every culture has to establish social rules if people are to get along halfway peacefully with each other. But rules alone are not enough. As individuals we also have to get things more or less straightened out with ourselves, have to be reasonably at peace with ourselves, otherwise the best rules are useless. And the culture should also contribute by pointing the way to a meaningful life.

It should help people develop the ability to recognize good and evil and decide against evil. What makes things extraordinarily difficult is the fact that the forces that trigger evil are neither good nor evil in themselves, they are namely the basic needs of body and soul. Only if we allow these forces to develop a life of their own will we be in danger, because they pull in different directions and all try and take precedence. The main challenge is to reconcile these divergent driving forces or balance them and make them productive for everyone.

Four impulses appear to me to be the dominant ones. There's the wish to keep our distance from other people — for a wide variety of reasons. For example, because we want to protect ourselves. Because in the company of others we must always expect onslaughts on our peace of mind, our pride, our self-satisfaction, which is a good reason to keep others at arm's length. In addition we need our freedom, scope for our experiments with ourselves, with life and with the world. We want to maintain our independence and demonstrate our self-reliance, so we must put others in their place and separate ourselves from them.

But as lovely as it is to be captain of your own ship, without a crew the ship would not set sail. We're dependent on others too, therefore it's just as important that we join up with them, even entrust ourselves to them and belong to them. Not only will this fulfill our desire for protection, it's the only way our pronounced need for recognition will be satisfied. Aside from this, as already mentioned, we strive for power. Conquering territory, defending territory is a primal impulse and an advantage simply because we have to maintain our freedom and it's easier to enforce our own claims from a position of power.

In a word, we're torn between the wish to earn the love of others and the need to show them that we can easily do without them. The art of living is therefore not least a balance between striving for independence and longing for protection. However, another fundamental and rather strange desire can also be observed: we want to stand out. We want to separate ourselves from the mass of similar beings. We want to be important, play a role, and be included in the circle of impressive people who are admired and envied by others. We want to be someone who can't be ignored, who has something to say and whose opinion counts. This primal impulse could also, like the others, be connected with the self-preservation instinct. Being important undoubtedly protects us against the risk of being simply blown away by life and going unsung; with an aura of importance we have less to worry about than someone who's barely known. But I don't think that's all there is to it. There's evidently pleasure associated with taking the life experiment far beyond merely asserting oneself and showing that one is not bound by the usual limitations of ordinary people, that one is as it were superior to everyone else. And we will encounter this strange claim to uniqueness with particular frequency in the context of the deadly sins.

Now it's a fact that these contrary impulses arise simultaneously in almost every life situation and clash with one other, so that we're constantly confronted with the question of whether to proceed alone or with others, operate with each other or against each other. To give a concrete example, when the bank I work in as an investment advisor is cheating its customers, do I go along with it or do I give notice? And these issues are not decided on a case-by-case basis as the person concerned thinks fit. They're decided by the basic personal attitude that has evolved in an individual over the years. Because at least with respect to the fundamental questions we form an opinion very early on about matters such as how much faith we can put in life, how threatening the world is, how dangerous our fellow human beings are, how much we should be afraid, and how we can banish this fear?

Our answers to such questions reflect our relationship to life. They shape our beliefs and our relationship to others and together form an attitude to life on which we largely base our decisions. It is then scarcely possible to make any corrections, because like all habits they create neural links in the brain that are reinforced and stabilized with frequent repetition. This is why such basic settings are tough and durable and with this I come back to the deadly sins.

It's easy to see how important the cultural environment is for our attitude to life. This is what largely determines whether we are able to tame and harmonize our contradictory impulses or whether one of these forces develops a life of its own, gains the upper hand, and destroys our internal balance. As individuals we would be faced with an impossible task if we had no cultural standards to guide us, if there were no traditions and general values to come to our aid. But what happens if a culture no longer sets standards for a meaningful life? When on the contrary it encourages and rewards even destructive and self-destructive basic attitudes?

I fear that such a way of life can be sure of a broad consensus, because the unleashing of individual drives is always felt to be liberating, and is often a pleasurable experience. A valve is opened and relief is obtained. The majority of the deadly sins are such valves: greed, anger, pride, and vainglory for example. A system that is based on deadly sins is therefore sure to be successful. It has an exciting effect because it makes self-control unnecessary and scorns all efforts to live in peace with ourselves and others. After all, the deadly sins also make us lose interest in others; our compassion dries up and we're dominated by a ruthless, ego-centered attitude. Basically they result in the numbing of our mental powers.

We long for self-assurance. We spend our lives trying to feel secure, trying to achieve a state of fearlessness and effortlessness, the blissful sense of floating above everything. We do all we can to reach this state and those who don't feel confident in themselves will make all the more effort to increase their external security, to make themselves invulnerable, to imagine themselves invincible, and maintain their place in the world by all the means at their disposal. This is the sense in which the deadly sins are to be understood, as strategies for achieving self-confidence single-handedly and usually at the cost of others.

Now that we've found out something about the causes and the nature of evil, I would like to focus on these strategies. I want now to talk about the impact of evil, with the deadly sins as guidelines. This is appropriate for the simple reason that in our day they have become very conspicuous. In addition, they've always been associated with social criticism: pride was a characteristic of the nobility, avarice and greed were attributed to the rich, while the poor were accused of envy. I will keep to the number seven specified by Gregory the Great but would like to adapt the traditional list to modern circumstances and therefore take over only five of the classical vices, namely envy, greed, pride, anger, and vainglory, renamed narcissism. The gaps should be filled with impatience and faithlessness. And as far as the term "deadly sins" is concerned — yes, although it's ambiguous and misleading, it's far more powerful than any of the alternatives. I would therefore like to retain it.

15

The root of all evil — envy

The explosive power of envy . . . I experienced it once. My aunt's will was spirited away by a cousin, and now the whole family were sitting together, with the wife of my cousin opposite me. I couldn't look at her, envy was written all over her face, which was actually distorted by greed and envy. Did the two really need everything from my aunt's legacy? This wasn't what it was about. They didn't want us to have anything. Under such circumstances, rifts are inevitable and one wonders whether envy creates anything apart from bitterness?

An age-old question. Of all the deadly sins, envy has always been the biggest enigma, because the intoxicating, impulsive, one is almost tempted to say lustiness of the other deadly sins is missing. It is a lonely, sad vice, a torment for everyone, but most of all for the envious themselves. No one gets anything out of it. In Ovid's *Metamorphoses* the appearance of the goddess of envy is repulsive: she dwells in a poor hovel, lives on snakes, has black teeth, and secretes bile. In a 17th-century painting, the allegorical figure of envy is even shown eating her own heart while her eyes seem to shoot poisoned arrows and her face is distorted by jealousy. What's so tempting, we might ask, what's the attraction of envy? But then we discover with amazement when we explore the matter further that as absurd as envy appears to be, no vice is more widespread or more feared, as if envy were a concentrated form of evil.

The evil eye that plays such an important role in magic is in fact the envious eye, the covetous or resentful eye that's cast on me and my possessions. According to popular belief, the look alone can do damage, and you can't be sufficiently on your guard against it; today in many countries people still protect themselves with amulets. In some cultures envy is even taken for granted, considered to be natural, and there's no such thing as an innocent look. Just noticing something can mean you want it, which is why in Arabic countries praise of an attractive object can easily be understood as a wish to be given it. "What a gorgeous ring," the guest says appreciatively without any ulterior motives and the host interprets this as "I would like you to give it to me . . ." The ring can then actually change hands as a result. Envy is taken into account right from the start and generosity is a strategy to take the sting out of this ubiquitous vice.

To see is to desire, the eye claims what it sees. Envy is in fact considered to be the quintessentially visual vice. While anger and greed make you blind, the envious eye is on the watch and the envious look sends poisoned arrows, although not in order to obtain something, only with destruction in mind. Envy also has good hearing. "We never answer the question 'How are you?' with 'very well' or 'great'," an Italian woman told me years ago. "We say, 'So-so'. We don't want to arouse envy. No one likes to hear how good another person feels, that makes people envious and they then wish you ill."

The evil eye, the malicious desire are enough. The envious person is credited with spoiling the happiness of others by willpower alone, without actively doing anything. No such uncanny power is attributed to any of the other deadly sins. None of them is so omniscient that one has to be continuously armed against it. There seems to be a real primal fear of envy.

Although envy follows an absurd logic. It goes like this: we have it good, we're satisfied — until another person has it better than we do. Now we also want to have it better than, or at least as good as the other person, if not a bit better. What we've had up to now is no longer good enough, we absolutely have to improve on the situation, keep our noses to the grindstone and work overtime, so that we have it good again ...

How can we possibly find this logic plausible?

"People can't endure seeing someone being promoted," says the Spanish writer Rafael Chirbes. Why? Because the successful person upstages me? Because he puts me to shame? But it's only unbearable if I feel small myself. If I permanently have the feeling of having missed out. And if I also deliberately look for opportunities to feel neglected and disadvantaged by comparing myself and my circumstances incessantly with others and their life situation — as if compelled to look for confirmation that I'm constantly subject to a kind of higher injustice. The question is: are we born disadvantaged? Is a major inferiority complex part of our basic make-up? And do we stop feeling small when we one day at last arrive in the upper echelons of society?

The fact is that the envious person presumes that the success of the other person wasn't fairly achieved. He doesn't see the other's achievement, talents or particular qualifications, he only sees manipulation, cunning, shamelessness, and undeserved luck. The successful person must have been devious, if nothing irregular had been going on, success would have come to the envious person. Even when this isn't possible, envy finds its victims. All those in public life must expect that the first false step will bring vituperation, verbal abuse, and mockery down upon them and that everyone is waiting to see them fall. Here the compassion that can usually expected from fellow human beings in similar circumstances is totally lacking. Because the unlucky public figure has had it far too good for far too long? Because people see this as compensatory justice?

But envy isn't only kindled by another's success. The most secret dissatisfaction we harbor is with our own appearance, and envy of another's beauty perhaps occurs even more frequently than envy of success, as if injustice were involved, as if the perfect looks of another were as little deserved as one's own average face. In the same way as small children constantly sense injustice, adults evidently also suspect they are being ignored or neglected and are plagued with self-doubt, asking what's wrong with me that I was denied what fell into others' laps? Envy boils down to an agonizing cry of Why him? Why her? Why not me?

And if you now look at what envy's aim is, what will finally satisfy it, there are two things: either the outdoing of the rival or the ruin of the same. Envy isn't necessarily aiming high. Since the rival is often not to be outdone, the envious person is satisfied with knowing that he or she is pursued by bad luck... and does everything possible to augment it. Thus we enter envy's own special territory, the domain of intrigue.

There are countless examples from administrative authorities, public offices where departments work against each other, shooting down suggestions, undermining initiatives, thwarting plans, and putting obstacles in the way of each other wherever possible. In everyday life envy pursues a strategy of attrition. It is a master of exerting power by means of hindrance. The same can even be experienced with friends. You have a project, you ask them to support you and pull a few strings, they also promise their support — and then behind your back do everything to make you look ridiculous and sabotage your project. Because even among friends there's the fear that the other person might cut a better figure than oneself and now envy becomes more attractive: through the satisfaction of successfully demolishing a competitor. The person who's been brought down can't outshine anyone, and how cheering it is to see him squirming, floundering, despairing, and finally giving up.

But it goes further than this. If envy has gone deep enough it can already take effect when my neighbor catches up with me. It may happen that I would rather wish him ill than wish myself well, that I would rather see him unhappy than myself happy. The English theologian John of Salisbury (1115-80) carries the absurdity of envy to extremes in the following fable. A king wants to grant a request to each of two men — one miserly, the other envious, in such a way that the one gets double what the other person wants. Expecting the double share, the miser lets the envious person ask first. He thinks about it for a long time and then asks to have an eye put out so that the other person loses both . . .

Here John of Salisbury describes the nature of envy very well. Envy doesn't just pervade all human relationships like a poison, it ultimately takes on the characteristic of absurd vengeance. Revenge for something the envied person never owed the envious one. Nevertheless, the envious person links his fate with the other person to the point where he accepts his own ruin if the other person also comes to grief. A kind of devilish energy seems to be concentrated in envy, something very close to senseless malice. And no reason in the world could stop it, because the envious person considers his envy justified, he's actually convinced he's the victim of higher injustice, of a fateful discrimination. But what peculiar sense of justice is involved here? Where does the claim of the envious person to the same fortune — and in the extreme case the same misfortune — as the envied person come from? And what is this strange contest really about?

One of the many remarkable scenes in the aforementioned Scorsese movie *The Wolf of Wall Street* runs as follows: the FBI investigator who's pursuing the fraudster Jordan Belfort visits him on his luxury yacht. Belfort is sunbathing on deck full of pride in his possession and puts up amiably with the accusations of the investigator — what can this little policeman do to a man who is successful at everything? Even personal insults go over his head, they don't touch him, he's protected by the shield of his success. But then when the investigator fails to admire the yacht, Belfort loses his composure. The disparagement of his showpiece pierces his heart. Why? Not only because his whole life model of greed for success is questioned, I suspect. But because this little official also refuses to recognize him as a child of fortune, as the darling of the gods, to use an old-fashioned term.

For the yacht doesn't simply make Belfort proud, it's more than a status symbol for him. At the moment when two contrary life models clash in the form of the fraudster and the investigator, the yacht is proof of how fate has favored him, a fact of which Belfort has been sure up until now. It's the symbol of his virtually metaphysical rank, which raises him far above the ordinary world of the investigator and his trivial notions of right and morality. No one can deny him his success. But his self-image as someone honored and blessed by fate can be destroyed and this is just what the little policeman has succeeded in doing. This brings us to the story of Cain and Abel, the classical drama of envy and jealousy.

The story of the fratricide comes in Genesis between the Fall of Man and the flood. Here at the beginning of the Old Testament everything is condensed, and the development of man is reduced to the key moments, related in short and concise episodes. The first human emotion we hear of is shame, through the awakening of conscience after the Fall. And immediately afterwards comes envy, which arises from the experience of having forfeited the right to divine favor and the desperate wish to regain this favor. The story goes as follows.

Cain and Abel, the sons of the first human couple, offer a sacrifice to God, each on his own altar. Cain is a crop farmer and offers the fruit of the ground. Abel is a sheep breeder and offers lambs. "And the Lord had regard for Abel and his offering, but for Cain and his offering he had no regard," it says laconically. Meaning simply that in Abel's case, the sacrifice fulfilled its purpose, and God gave him the desired success, whereas Cain's sacrifice was in vain, and he was denied comparable success. So Cain was very angry and his countenance fell, the narrator continues, everything in him rebelled against the supposed injustice of God and overwhelmed with anger he killed his brother Abel.

Once again, at the beginning of Genesis, a basic human motive is exposed, and envy is such a motive. The real point of this story, however, is man's inescapable connectedness with God as demonstrated by, of all things, a deadly sin. This shows that although envy is so powerfully inflamed by the things of the visible world, this is the least of what it's about. The point isn't even that Cain begrudges his brother his financial success, the love of his wife or his many children. What he does however greatly begrudge him is his primacy with God, his preference by the heavenly powers which is visibly expressed in his success. In modern terms one could say it's not the other person's Ferrari one envies, it's the — undeserved — luck of being able to afford a Ferrari in the first place. The first murder therefore occurs out of jealousy of a competitor who's favored more by the divinity than the murderer. Cain asks the perpetual question of a child who believes he has reason to feel neglected. Why is he loved more than me? How has *he* deserved his good luck, how have *I* deserved my bad luck?

So basically Cain rebelled against God. Killing Abel, the fortunate one, was an emergency solution, a kneejerk reaction caused by the unbearable disappointment at being ignored by God. Getting rid of the more successful competitor for divine favor is probably logical in the light of envy: it's done in the hope of taking his place with God and inheriting the rival's success. And even if we don't recognize it nowadays, our self-esteem is as dependent as ever on evidence that we're favored by fate. When we always come off second best in life, we're forced to believe in the injustice of a higher power if we are to continue to believe in ourselves.

Although even those who to our minds have risen very high in society aren't spared envy. Because even in the highest economic circles, where the air is already thin, there will always be someone who has risen a step higher, so that even here the extra meter of a sailing yacht or the extra square meter of a villa or its grounds will matter. We always draw the short straw. This explains the omnipotence of envy and the power of the despair it gives rise to.

Envy and greed are the driving forces of our economic system, as London's mayor Boris Johnson said. Envy is at least in reality too destructive to do much for an economic system. Yet Johnson is right because envy has a second side that's highly beneficial to the economy. Even successful people need envy. Their happiness is derived not least from the malicious glee at having left the others behind and knocked them down a peg, and their pride of ownership is often fed as much by the envy of the losers as by consciousness of their own competence. I'm allied with the powers of fate, I'm the darling of the gods – such feelings keep a high-flyer like Jordan Belfort going, as long as no humble FBI investigator turns up and refuses to pay the accustomed homage of the envious.

I'm willing to concede that it must be an uplifting feeling to be assured of the envy of one's fellows. Nevertheless, it's fundamentally erroneous to see an increase in wealth and power as confirmation of one's uniqueness. And this gives rise to a second fallacy, namely considering an enviable life to be more desirable than a happy life. Because being envied is not the same as being happy; nowadays the two things are too readily confused.

"My husband and I live a life of which others can only dream. We are happy," I read in an interview with two successful people, who posed in photos in front of what was indeed imposing evidence of wealth. The article in itself showed that the two coveted recognition and envious admiration and my impression is that, like these two successful people, many others also picture an enviable life when they think of a happy life. An error, as I said.

Because in order to live an enviable life you must score, show off, boast of a perfect career, a perfect physique, and perfect children, pile it on and show what you have, and first you must really have a lot, which in turn means hard graft, raking in the money and piling up acquisitions. At some point you may indeed succeed in impressing others and basking in their envy. You would thus have achieved your goal and usually happiness has fallen by the wayside in the process.

In order to be happy, you don't need everything. Envious

glances can be exhilarating but they are dearly bought. You've made yourself dependent on the assessment of your fellows and must now always put on the same show, must mobilize all your energies to maintain the same façade of happiness, no matter how black things look behind it. So you lose sight of yourself. The only thing that matters is keeping up the pretense of having fate on your side, so that the pursuit of happiness becomes a farce, a performance for the cheap and of course also the expensive seats — it's not for nothing that all the pictures from the world of the rich and beautiful people remind you of stage scenery, theater, and play-acting. True happiness, however, is not having to pretend. True happiness is being independent of the judgment of the audience, is the luxury of being able to be honest with yourself and others. And happy people, incidentally, know no envy. The theater of the enviable life makes no impression on them. They live their lives for themselves, not for an audience.

In one respect, the strange deadly sin of envy comes very close to the truth. For the longed-for good fortune of envious people goes beyond what they can achieve on their own, it's only possible as a gift, as a moment of fulfillment. This shows that the envious are actually on the right path, because in order to have the desired exhilarating effect, good fortune must come unexpectedly. What can be planned and earned, demanded or claimed doesn't make us happy, for the simple reason that it doesn't make us grateful. But happiness and gratitude are one and the same thing and the moment of gratitude is the moment of fulfillment.

From this perspective, the dream of the envious of an unexpected fortune falling into their laps came true for my cousin and his wife with the inheritance. They might have been satisfied. But envy isn't so easily pleased. Scarcely is the goal within reach than it turns into resentment of everyone who could contest this good fortune. Incapable of gratitude, it insists on the exclusivity of its good fortune and so envy has always inevitably changed happiness into unhappiness.

16

Who can outdo Bill Gates? — greed

Envy is the foremost of all vices. Because it doesn't permanently have to be a secret, damaging feeling of indignation that one is being treated with indifference by the forces of fate. Envy can erupt like a disease after a certain period of incubation and then turn into greed. In this respect Boris Johnson is right: there's no greed without envy. And greed can definitely be relied upon. It's an infectious disease.

With greed envy becomes active. The oppressive feeling of apparently having nothing to claim leads at most to spitefulness but in general paralyzes one's forces. Under certain circumstances this bitterness can change into its euphoric opposite, namely the exhilarating certainty of being entitled to literally everything and being able to enforce this boundless claim against all resistance, rules, and reason. Individual cases of this have occurred in every age. In the past, however, greed went with power and opportunity, as is shown for example in the gold fever of the conquistadors and Californian gold miners, in the plunder of conquered cities and territories or in the pomp of secular rulers and church dignitaries.

But never before has greed spread through an entire society and culture. Our dismay at the processes we've been witnessing for about a decade is caused by the realization that everyone is now a gambler. The world has been transformed into a single vast gambling hall and there no longer seem to be any valid rules and principles with which the claim of everyone to everything could be refuted. What now seems to be the rule is that people in the top positions grant themselves fantastic salaries until they overstep the mark, then cash in again massively and subsequently defraud the state of tax. And scarcely has the annoyance over such practices subsided in the lower than the culprits advance to become models.

Or may one in this case no longer speak of culprits? Has evil disappeared here too, because it's also become a common practice, accepted by everyone? And what was that about the dramatic aspect of evil? As spectators, it fascinates and excites us. Could it be that in our media-dominated world we've indeed all become observers, and those insatiable managers, bankers, and traders merely provide a spectacle by presenting the primary vice of envy in its most dramatic and therefore most attractive form — as greed? Then they wouldn't be offenders. Then they would justly have the name with which they evidently feel most comfortable. Then they would be players, actors, and gamblers rolled into one. In that case it would be useless to still distinguish between good and evil. Looked at like this, all that would be important would be whether you leave the stage as a winner or a loser.

If we're honest, we have to admit that we're not totally ungrateful for this spectacle of greed. We may find top German managers who travel to London in order to sue for their astronomical bonus remunerations contemptible, but on the whole disgust and fascination probably balance each other out, because like pride, greed is one of the flamboyant deadly sins, and by contrast with envy we're easily convinced of its advantages. We also believe, not necessarily in the happiness which wealth promises, but in the significance of wealth. And aside from this it could flatter us to be included in the spectacle of greed, because all the efforts are undertaken for the benefit of us, the spectators.

Of course it has its ridiculous sides, this play entitled I've made it, I've outstripped you. When it's no longer about enjoying individual possessions but simply about impressing — whether it's with the art on the walls, the brand new kitchen or the motor yacht in Monaco harbor, the most important thing being that whatever it is, it's expensive. But that's how it is: money must be made visible through the things it can buy. As long it's still in the bank, it's invisible, so that for the public it doesn't exist and is therefore practically worthless. As soon as it takes the form of a motor yacht, however, it comes alive and goes on stage, and then the curtain opens on the individual's wealth and the play begins . . . And we ordinary people find ourselves obediently participating and immediately converting the yacht back into money: I see, that's two million floating out there. And when we consider the estimated price of the old masters, the high-performance kitchen or the luxurious yacht to reflect the outstanding qualities of their owner, when we see these things not as status symbols but as power symbols, signs of strength, and supremacy which identify their owner as an excellent, truly outstanding human being, then we've fulfilled our purpose as spectators.

Global players can certainly only impress their equals with facts and figures. Here what matters is one's place on the ranking list, one's position within the hierarchy of the super-rich, and the question is thus who can outdo Bill Gates? As far as everyone else is concerned, however, the purpose of the absurd wealth is the self-representation, self-revelation of the rich, which is why as many people as possible must notice the newly acquired Maserati — look at this, I can afford this too! And it works. There have probably never ever been so many people who've believed in the statement made by wealth. We're easier than ever to convince of the singularity and happiness of a person on the basis of the external attributes of success. It's amazing, because I'm sure that our deepest longing won't have changed — the desire to convince as a person. To be loved for our own sake.

It's our perpetual hope that others may discover something in us. Something exceptional that we're perhaps not aware of ourselves. A unique talent, a unique ability or a particular likeable character trait. Something that makes us more attractive than we consider ourselves to be, our real selves as it were, which incidentally can also suffer under our actual life circumstances, the limitations imposed from outside. In any case our true selves would expand and become much grander if we were freed from the bonds of the given circumstances, if we could shed this tight, ugly skin — in other words, if we could achieve a breakthrough.

This breakthrough can occur in the form of professional success in acknowledgement of our qualities in a particular field. It can also take the form of admission to the more exclusive circles or clubs with all the resulting possibilities of development. This will be associated with increased respect, power, and money and not least with a new self image: I'm the one who's made it. Nothing can be said against this. This advancement would have been achieved through work and effort and there's a good chance our self-confidence and self-satisfaction have increased too so that we could almost certainly do without all the spectacular forms of self-representation. Our whole life would already sufficiently express our true self.

However, there's a great temptation as soon as the breakthrough is achieved to make use of the visible attributes of wealth to leave no one in any doubt about our superb real selves. The temptation is great because these attributes of wealth are the most efficient form of self-presentation and we're now all groomed for efficiency and effectiveness. Nothing can be gained with inner wealth if you want to have an instantaneous effect on people; intellectual depth, for example, can only be discovered by talking, requires a lengthy, possibly strenuous discussion with the person concerned and will only be appreciated by someone who has a feel for it. It can't be converted at a glance into euros, and the mind is in any case much harder to convince than the eyes. With the expressiveness of wealth you get ahead faster, also because this language is now understood and spoken by everyone. My outrageously expensive shoes thus now show what is in me. My belongings reveal my inner life and my Maserati is the image of myself. They might be images of my inner life that have ossified into façades — but they nevertheless express my true self.

What I wonder is that whether in this case human beings must in turn be prepared to be converted into euros or dollars. And would it bother them?

"This vice especially is to be cut out of the monastery by the roots . . . no one has anything as his own — anything whatever, whether books or tablets or pen or whatever it may be . . . but if anyone is caught indulging in this most wicked vice, let him be admonished once and a second time. If he fails to amend, let him undergo punishment."

Thus it is written with rare intransigence in the Monastery Rule of our founder St. Benedict. Anyone who entered the monastery had to renounce all belongings; Benedict was in no doubt about this, and the regulation is also followed to this day by all other orders. Greed in all its manifestations was for him the primary evil of mankind and at the same time the hallmark of civilization. As a true son of the ancient world, he abhorred everything uncontrolled, immoderate or excessive, and saw it as an expression of instability unworthy of man as the image of God. The greed for money and possessions was for him the epitome of all the wrong paths human beings can set foot upon. When he set up the Rule for the monastic life he had in mind a godly and dignified counterworld whose highest principle was moderation. Greed should not even be given a chance.

He modelled his monastic community incidentally on ordinary society, on the family. He appreciated the sense of community that is most likely to develop in a group of manageable size, but he also certainly saw the family as one of the few areas where things and services were not given for money. Surprisingly this has remained so to this day. In our time, the family is probably the only place not dominated by the price–performance relationship. That's why it demonstrates perfectly how money interferes with human relationships and I shall try to illustrate this with an example.

The price–performance relationship can confidently be considered to be practically the ultimate unit of value, and meanwhile literally the whole world can be measured by it. Nevertheless, it wouldn't occur to us to pay our mother for cleaning our shoes or serving us meals. Outside the family or circle of friends it would be a normal service and have to be paid for, but the service of a mother has no price in this sense. It has a value, but this cannot be expressed in figures. We would find it inappropriate, downright offensive, and we see that here money has completely lost its exchange value. Why?

Because here feelings, emotional relationships come into play. And when money tries to invade our emotional world we erect a barrier against it. Suddenly we realize that money is more than a means of payment. It's for example also a means of buying freedom from the feeling of thankfulness and connectedness that I owe somebody who's rendered me a service or done something nice for me. Money liberates me from all emotional obligations, it objectifies human relationships, it shifts them into the impersonal realm of cost–benefit thinking, and now we understand why mothers don't get offered and don't take money for cleaning shoes: objectifying an emotional relationship in this way would be brutal, offensive, and even humiliating.

What we're now experiencing is that money as a medium of exchange has crept into almost all areas of life. Almost everything has its price, almost everything can be had for money. Basically it's practical — who would want to hug the butcher for every cutlet? Apart from the fact that he wouldn't hand it over for a hug. Nevertheless, a world dominated by calculation constantly gets colder, more insensitive, and to put it bluntly coarser, and we usually only notice this when a boss justifies his condescending behavior to his subordinates by saying, "But I pay them for it." Personally it's for this reason that I like going to parts of the world that aren't governed solely by money, in particular Africa. Here someone from the West who's accustomed to whipping out a purse on every occasion can have some irritating encounters.

Imagine that you're traveling on a country road in Africa towards a village and see a woman on the roadside waving to you in your car and indicating with gestures that she's inviting you to her house. You stop and you and your companion are indeed invited to drink tea with her, although you haven't met before. And while she's preparing the tea you wonder what this woman wants. Why is she doing this? Presumably out of hospitality and because it's something special to have European guests; Europeans seldom come to this area. Apparently she's enjoying spending time with us and is happy to be able to do us a favor with her tea. But can she even afford it? The hut in which we sit looks poor . . . Then when you say goodbye you offer her a little money for the delicious tea and the pleasant time spent under her roof. Then her smile disappears and she coolly rejects your offer.

Yes, in that world the brutal, humiliating nature of money is still felt. It's still a world of kindness, not a world of calculation, not a world of "you scratch my back, I'll scratch yours." The founder of the African monastery of Agbang once said to me, " We Africans aren't familiar with the protection of vested rights. It's African to share . . ." The invitation of that woman was an act of kindness, an act of sharing, and this kindness becomes devalued if it's compensated for in money. Here the moments of emotional connectedness are more important than the prospect of a few quick dollars, here people can still distinguish between the value and the price of an item. Much more than we can, anyway.

I'm reminded of the photo of an old black American, probably taken in the 30s of the last century. I found it in a book by the French philosopher Roland Barthes, and it's unforgettable for me for the same reason that Barthes included it in his book. "No lust for power" was all he put under the photo, but these words sum up his and my amazed reaction. This man looks at us without demanding anything. This is immediately noticeable. From the enclosed space of his own inner world he looks at the camera completely at one with himself and with the world, utterly unassuming and undemanding and at perfect peace. In this face modesty is clearly expressed as a spiritual force and as inconspicuous as this person is otherwise, this look is unforgettable because it contrasts blatantly with the usual way of perceiving the world.

Not very long ago I saw the letters of a German who had spent some months in New York in the 1950s. The letters were addressed to his wife and New York was new for him, so there should have been a lot to report, but surprisingly he had no eye for this exciting city. The most frequent word in his letters was "opportunity." He judged situations, people, and the totally different life in New York solely according to the respective opportunities they provided to establish business connections. He saw the world solely through the lens of his financial interests. Everything else, the real New York, must have seemed superfluous to him. Evidently all that mattered to him were the exploitable aspects of this city.

Greed does indeed make you blind, because greedy people don't contemplate. They don't let an image work on them, they don't want to get an overall impression, they certainly don't want get to the bottom of things — they're content with the surface and at most sort their impressions into the categories of useful and useless. The greedy survey the world without gathering any information other than that relating to possible profit. Useful facts are registered and stored, useless facts overlooked. Everything is explored in terms of the opportunities for gain and such people ask themselves constantly how they can change a given situation to their advantage. Looked at in this way, namely from the point of view of greed, the picture of the black American would only suggest submissiveness, at best resignation to fate, and a regrettable lack of ambition and drive. But what would this man on the other hand think of people who are only wired for intervention and the weighing up of opportunities? Whose focus is increasingly narrowing?

Let's come finally to the crucial question of whether money makes you happy or unhappy. It's easy to answer. Money can make you happy if you have none or only a little. But money devalues the world. The more money you have, the cheaper the world becomes, the more it loses its value and meaning, until everything is available to you and nothing more attracts you. Aside from that, if a high income were important for personal satisfaction, monks and nuns should be profoundly dissatisfied. However, all my experiences are to the contrary and all surveys indicate that dissatisfaction is highest in the richest countries. The happiness potential of money seems to be used up rather rapidly, which renders the behavior of greedy people pointless. But what drives them?

Let's look at gluttony, a classic failure of self-control. You neglect yourself, you lose all sense of moderation, you fill your plate six times because it's free or everything is offered for the price of 6 euros 50 cents: all you can eat, whenever you want. Those who do this aren't doing it to satisfy their hunger. They want to savor the good fortune of finding a special offer. Here it's not about the thing itself, the enjoyment of a tasty meal, for example. What is irresistible is rather the fact of having to pay nothing or significantly less and thus experiencing unmerited good fortune, which in turn signifies being singled out by fate. Even in such a trifling case, the good fortune granted is associated with a small, positive revaluation of one's person and it's therefore necessary to take ample advantage of the given opportunity.

How much happier will unmerited good fortune then make the gambler, the global player or the trader who plays with billions of dollars or euros: this enormous profit, this immense wealth — I didn't earn it! It fell into my lap! A gift from heaven! I've turned the world order on its head, I've invalidated the merit principle, I can make it rain money on me without lifting a finger — what a feeling of freedom, superiority, and omnipotence this experience must give them. It's no longer about the pleasure in any particular things, it's no longer a matter of enjoying life, it's all about self-satisfaction, about being intoxicated with one's own magnificence as the favorite of the gods. Here greed has taken on a life of its own and become the real meaning of life.

We are evidently living in a world that has gone mad. It may seem touchingly ingenuous to try once again to be reasonable about this, but we don't actually need much to be happy, nor is it our possessions on which we really love. What would most people save first from a fire? The photo albums. Those things that contain our adventures and experiences, that are associated with irretrievable moments of happiness and therefore seem priceless to us, because they don't lose their value. Our need for material goods is limited and our contentedness depends much more on what could be called inner wealth. Looked at objectively, the spectacle of unlimited greed is thus nothing but insane. But the most frightening thing about this is that this insanity is entirely logical in itself.

Because contentedness means at some point having enough and knowing when this point has arrived. It means sooner or later taking the pressure off and enjoying what's there. And this is precisely what would spell the end of an economic system which promises permanent growth and has to keep this promise under all circumstances. Satisfaction would make this system collapse. There must be no "enough." The better we have it, the more threatening the situation and perhaps the last chance of such an economic system is indeed to assume completely irrational dimensions, abolish the merit principle, and offer the ultimate most irresistible incentive, the self-intoxication of a "master of the universe." Excess with its lure of megalomania and total irresponsibility. Or in other words: the good fortune that comes to me entirely unearned, awarded me by fate not for my efforts but solely because of the person I am. With which we are already within the sphere of the third deadly sin.

17

Life as a talent show — narcissism

"My son doesn't have to pick up waste paper off the classroom floor. Not even if he dropped it," says a mother to the teacher.

I haven't made this up either. And as far as I know, teachers are increasingly hearing things like this from parents. You would rather just shake your head and forget about it. But what you've heard sticks in your mind and you ask, for example, whether this mother wants her son to be an irresponsible little monster? Or does she see her offspring as some kind of demigod? He can't be an ordinary person in her eyes. Does she herself perhaps feel like a demigod, who makes use without further ado of her privileges and special authority when faced with inconvenient reality? There must in any case be something special about mother and son.

It's not easy to say exactly what the two sentences quoted above smack of. Hubris? Self-satisfied ignorance? Egocentrism? Narcissism? The mother's utterances allow for all these interpretations, but narcissism is probably the most apt. This term embraces everything that comes under the classical deadly sin of vanity, and in addition, no other term is more suitable as the hallmark of the present, or so often used to characterize our time.

If the ancient Greeks had known what the myth of Narcissus would come to represent approximately two and a half millennia later . . . For what excesses of self-love it would become the symbol . . . But everything is in fact contained in this little story: Narcissus, young and beautiful, is out hunting when he catches sight of his reflection in the water of a pool. He's delighted and immerses himself in this image, as it were drinking in his own beauty; he forgets about the world around him and can't tear himself away, until a goddess redeems him from his narcissistic torpor and transforms him into a flower, a narcissus. In another version of the myth, Narcissus, steeped in his own incomparability, rejects all who court him and is the archetypical person incapable of love and commitment, self-sufficient, and too good for everyone else. In the Palazzo Barberini in Rome he's perfectly depicted by Caravaggio as a fully closed system: the face and arms of the real Narcissus merge seamlessly with his reflection in the water, his self-love circulating in an eternal cycle through his body. A magnificent painting.

And now the stage is set for the circus of self-deification, vanity fair, the narcissism of our time.

Let's begin with the vanity of see and be seen — in Bayreuth, Salzburg, and Vienna, in Monaco at the Formula 1 race and at the Baur au Lac Hotel on Lake Zurich, places where the beautiful, rich, and important celebrate themselves. Good luck to them. What I always find amazing is what people wear on their lapels at public receptions and how important it is to have one's photo in the paper afterwards and to be mentioned in the welcome address beforehand. And then there's the bad habit of the guests who after listening to a speech then continue with a speech of their own . . . Well, that's the age-old striving for recognition, and it doesn't have to make a person unlikable. Vanity in my opinion is not a serious vice: however, in Rome I'm used to people preening themselves with their invisible laurels. I would nevertheless like to point out something in this context: lack of vanity is by the same token a great, outstanding virtue, and demands respect, especially in the case of people with outstanding abilities. By avoiding a small vice one can acquire great virtue, which is all the more valuable for its rarity.

We first encounter the actual narcissist universe, however, in the relationship of parents to their children. Whenever I talk to teachers, educators, as well as parents and astute observers of our daily lives, I get the impression that many parents are deliberately bringing their children up to be inconsiderate and over-sensitive. In any case, this is the only possible result of an upbringing which prevents children from being forced to face reality. Three examples from everyday life in Germany will be sufficient to illustrate this.

Continuing the theme with which I began, a mother on the tram says to an old man who is unsteady on his feet, "My child mustn't stand." The child, a ten-year-old girl, remains sitting and instead a Turkish woman with a small child on her arm offers the man her seat ... And again, a father whose son continuously disturbs lessons is asked by the teacher to exert a moderating influence on him. The father refuses, saying that his son has the right to develop freely. And as a final example again taken from school, it increasingly happens that children with no self-control, who can't or don't want to follow the lessons, are declared by their parents to be intellectual high-flyers because their behavior can only be explained by the fact that they're particularly gifted ...

That should suffice. It could be said that these parents have forgotten that their responsibility is to educate their children, which isn't surprising in a world that has committed itself to forgetting. But it does surprise us, because apparently the parents are also living in a world of illusion, a world in which one's own flesh and blood is quite extraordinary and can therefore simply only be admired. I suspect that this is the world of winners programmed for success, in which, as we have seen, the question of good and evil no longer arises. According to a very strange theory of evolution, the children of such parents are already born with the aura of success. They are thus sure to rise rapidly to the top unless a narrow-minded and resentful society puts obstacles in their way. Obstacles in the form of school marks and a behavioral code, for example.

Children have always had to be responsible for realizing the — unfulfilled — dreams of their parents. The latter's own greatness would then be demonstrated in the next generation — people used to have a lot more time. But now we have something new. While people used to say our children should have it better, today they say my child should have it as easy as possible, right from the beginning. The happiness of my child is therefore paramount, and woe betide anyone who doesn't recognize his or her exceptional status.

Thus we are experiencing how the lack of seriousness of the Global Player has spread into every aspect of life, even the most personal relationships: our whole life is a game where there are only winners and losers and undeserved good fortune is the best and only desirable gratification. Reality must of course be blended out in the process, because the desired state of self-intoxication is only possible in a world of illusion. Again we hear the voice of Gordon Gekko in Oliver Stones' movie Money Never Sleeps, which in the meantime is resounding from everywhere: "Can't you understand? It's not about money, [about achievement, concrete goals, and identifiable wishes, we should add here] — it's about the game."

It's the game of Narcissus who's intoxicated by his own perfection, who forgets the world around him and basically finds everyone else aggravating. The parents in the above examples are in my opinion behaving with the narcissistic arrogance of people who see themselves reflected in their children like Narcissus in the water of the pool. The psychological explanation for this might for example be that the more the family loses its natural identity, and even forfeits its special legal status, the more it takes on a transfiguring gloss. It's possible that from an emotional point of view it's entering a sphere outside of reality. However, there's some evidence that the modern concept of family on the contrary reflects an economic reality, which is based — to quote Boris Johnson for the last time — on envy and greed.

"I don't have to worry. My father's always there with his wallet."

Utterances like this from a 14-year-old make you afraid that in many cases the family has become a school of narcissism. For narcissists always assume that the world fulfills their wishes without them having to contribute anything or take responsibility. Other people simply owe them their love, since they were born perfect; they don't have to prove their uniqueness or make any effort. But narcissists must put themselves on display. They must flaunt themselves, so that the world has the opportunity to admire them. And that's the real purpose of their existence: admiration and applause. They would be nothing without applause. They are immediately deflated when no one notices them.

So adolescent narcissists put themselves forward. They put themselves on display on the Internet or in talent and self-revelation shows like a product in a shop window and think incessantly about how to beautify themselves to ensure the applause never ends. Show what you have to offer — this is a maxim of the economy and people live accordingly: let yourself be seen, undress yourself, showcase yourself. The entire half-naked culture of the West follows this law. In its advanced stage, narcissism views the whole of life as a talent show and at this point it becomes a deadly sin.

Although I have to admit that it's not so easy in this context to talk about a deadly sin. Not as easy in any case as with envy and greed, which are obviously highly troublesome vices, and even Narcissus in the ancient myth is by no means wicked or dangerous. But he's unfit for life. He falls for an illusion which ultimately deprives him of the will to live. He no longer relates to reality and dies inside — nothing touches him, nothing moves him, nothing matters to him except himself. And when we remember that the deadly sins are basically wrong paths that human beings take in their search for happiness, this would give narcissism a place of honor in the catalog of deadly sins because it infallibly makes people unhappy. I would like to go into this aspect in greater detail.

Narcissists needs a tailor-made environment. Although they parade all their imperfections to their audience, are absurdly proud of their faults, neuroses, and intolerable character traits; at the same time they interpret any criticism as an attack on their personality, because their complacency is just a façade. They've never learned to put up resistance and to suffer defeat; their self-confidence depends on the favor of their public and in the face of hostility they give up. Narcissists thus don't like it when their feeling of stupendousness is undermined by people who don't think they're so great. In addition, they're also offended by everything that runs contrary to their expectations — hard working conditions, long working hours, and the behavior of other people for example.

In order for them to be happy, everyone has to pander to their wishes. People don't usually automatically do that. For this reason, narcissists are not capable of a lasting relationship — sooner or later they'll be dissatisfied with any partner and lose interest in him or her. These loners unable or unwilling to commit are well on the way to becoming the prototype of our time, and as is their nature, they consider these failings to be a sign of strength, as if they had a special talent for freedom and independence. Whereas what's happened is that they've lost the capacity for solidarity — they can't bear anything that's dissimilar to them and can't be expected to change. Basically they're terrified of anything unfamiliar, they can't do anything with it and they want things to be the same forever — what they want is themselves. Narcissists are the epitome of infertile, sterile human beings, and they're multiplying rapidly.

In 1953, psychologists asked young people in Germany, whether they thought they were important. 12 percent said yes. When the test was repeated in 2007, 88 percent of the young Germans thought they were important. Twenge and Campbell, two psychologists in the USA, found the same thing. They conducted a long-term study to find out whether students attributed exceptional gifts to themselves — the various self-evaluation alternatives culminated in the statement "If I ruled the world, it would be a better place." Up to the year 2000, the answers indicated a realistic self-image; since then the number of those who consider themselves capable of anything has skyrocketed. "Narcissism has increased like obesity," wrote Twenge and Campbell.

Feelings of infantile omnipotence are spreading. In the meantime, the entire Western world is characterized by narcissism, an exaggerated opinion of oneself combined with self-doubt, which is alleviated only by the permanent acknowledgement of others. In this way, modern human beings have become unprecedentedly dependent on everything that might make them attractive and enviable. They increasingly lose sight of themselves and live in an unreal world, vulnerable to any form of self-deception. Among the consequences are an inexorable aesthetic comparison competition in which more and more people consider themselves ugly.

The self-optimization mania, the desperate battle against age, the whole repertoire of styling measures that people hope will change them from inconspicuous to conspicuous beings — these are all signs of an unhappy society that's been subjected to the unattainable ideal of physical perfection. This rebellion against fate has developed tragic aspects, because after every cosmetic operation the other physical shortcomings are even more noticeable, and no anti-aging cream can ever halt the aging process. Why does the body cult then continue?

Not out of self-love, I suspect, more likely out of a profound helplessness. With their addiction to admiration, narcissists inevitably come into conflict with themselves: they must separate their body from their ego and downgrade it to an object; they look at their body from outside through the eyes of others and ask themselves incessantly how their body is judged by their fellow human beings. Can they present themselves to others or not? Their happiness depends to a large extent on whether their body is considered attractive. Because the body comparison competition can never be won, this way of looking at things undoubtedly means that fewer and fewer people feel satisfied with their physical appearance. Doctors and psychologists are in any case observing an alarming increase of aversion to one's own body in both men and women.

There's no escape from this trap. One can't imagine Narcissus as a bent old man. As long as we seriously dream of an Elysium where age and sickness are eliminated, in which everyone remains beautiful, desirable, and successful, we'll have to keep company with Narcissus by the side of the pool.

Stopping time. Clinging to the here and now. Controlling everything, especially one's body, age, and lifespan. I see that as a sign of a culture where death has the last word. Now the future we've committed ourselves to with all its consequences has proven to be the ultimate nightmare: we see a skull and make panic-stricken efforts to bring the lost paradise from the afterlife into this life. Maybe we actually want nothing more ardently than to transform ourselves into demigods, into creatures who don't have to pick up waste paper from the classroom floor, and never have to learn to look with equanimity at their wrinkles in the mirror. Or could we imagine being able to bear this?

18

Let's build a tower — hubris

In German hubris has many names: pride, imperiousness, thirst for glory, megalomania, presumptuousness, and arrogance. Milder forms of hubris are described as an exaggerated opinion of oneself, haughtiness, and pretension. These character traits have already been encountered in the last chapter, and narcissism and hubris do in fact overlap. However, there's a fundamental difference between them.

While narcissism was relatively less significant as a vice for a long time and only started to become prominent about two decades ago, hubris has been always closely associated with the history of the human race. And it's even more than this: both in Greek myths and the Old Testament hubris is quite simply the root of evil and simultaneously the force behind everything. The church father Augustine considered hubris to be an integral part of the human character — after the Fall of Man, he said, it became second nature to us. And the writer Egon Friedell (1878–1938) stated categorically in his monumental *Cultural History of the Modern Era*, "The basic instinct of man is imperiousness. He wants to rule over the dead and the living, bodies and souls, the future and the past."

Nevertheless, hubris doesn't seem to have such undisputed domination over human beings as this suggests. Sometimes it's still overtaken by greed, and in the past pride and greed alternated as the first on the list of deadly sins according to the prevailing attitude of the time. Whenever people argued about what drove individuals to seek dominance, they certainly talked about hubris, as illustrated by the great rulers and tyrants, and about the "all consuming greed for gold" as it was manifested by the conquistadors. But can this question ever be decided? And if so, what arguments can be used?

As we have seen, the early Christians had a particular aversion to greed, probably mainly because greed for money and possessions bind people most strongly to the material world, and this was what they were supposed to triumph over. In addition, it must have originally been a greater temptation than pride — the communities consisted predominantly of ordinary people and their precarious situation in the Roman Empire gave them little opportunity for pride. When in the 4th century Christianity became a recognized religion, conditions changed. The greed for positions, prestige, and power, and the striving for a successful career and recognition evidently endangered the Christian ideals even more than greed; in any case, under the influence of important church teachers such as Augustine and Gregory the Great, hubris moved to first place among the deadly sins, a position it maintained until the 13th century. But then, as a side effect of the economic upswing in Europe, greed came powerfully into play again, and took on such repulsive forms that it was once again seen as an even greater danger for the soul. The aversion to the rampant greed of this time is reflected in particular in the person of St. Francis of Assisi and the founding of mendicant orders. Greed then remained at the top of the list and developments in the following centuries evidently provided no reason to displace it again.

And what about today? It's difficult to decide. The 20th century may well be called the century of hubris, the epoch in which megalomania celebrated the most horrific triumphs; the 21th century, however, promises to become the century of greed. Perhaps it really is the case that over the centuries it's sometimes pride and sometimes greed that becomes paramount. But before we leave this question, I would like to look once again at what Greek mythology and the Bible have to say. They at least always have clear answers to fundamental questions.

What alarmed the ancient Greeks more than anything else was not greed, but hubris, reaching for the stars. Because this was where the territory of the gods began, who were intent on keeping their distance from people, regarded the goings-on on earth with suspicion and placed strict limits on the ambitious among mortals. Constantly concerned that human beings might get above themselves, "the gods traverse the states and cities to look at the iniquity and piety of the people," as it is written in the Odyssey. In other words, they were continuously checking whether the people were exercising some restraint on their lofty ambitions, in particular their most foolhardy desire, which was to wrest their fate from the gods and take it into their own hands. The God of the Old Testament also feared the same thing, namely a torrent of uncontrollable human self-will after Adam and Eve had eaten from the tree of knowledge. "See the man has become like one of us . . ." he noted and he intended with the banishment from paradise to put human beings in their place.

In both cases, it looks as if human beings and the celestial powers mutually distrust each other. People refuse to tolerate intervention from above and seek to determine their destiny alone; the celestial powers want to prevent precisely this and put a stop to all excessive high-handedness. Why? The ancient Greeks suspected that the gods prevented human beings from realizing their great plans out of jealousy. And surprisingly, modern atheism has the same criticism of every kind of belief: God patronizes people, withholds freedom from them and prevents them from developing to the full.

This isn't even wrong. This is actually at the heart of every religion, namely the insight that it isn't good for people to gain too much power over themselves and their fellows. This reflects a healthy skepticism obtained from bitter experience about the ability of human beings to set themselves limits. Once in possession of power, whether political, economic or intellectual, they tend to make irresponsible use of their freedom, defy all the precepts of humanity, and shrink from no act of madness. Who's going to call them to order if not the gods, if not God? Psychologically speaking, every religion is indebted to the horror of one's own immoderation and the belief in a higher power who sets the reasonable limits that people can't set themselves. Seen like this, religions can be understood as a preventive measure against megalomania, and hubris on the other hand as the central driving force of human beings, so powerful that the most massive bulwark has to be erected against it.

Hubris surpasses all the deadly sins. It has nothing of the banality of envy, greed, and narcissism. It stimulates people to grow beyond themselves, to reach for the stars and, as it's said in Genesis, become like God. Like all the driving forces of human action, it's neither good nor evil in itself, but only hubris has this exhilarating, world-shaking power that commands reverential admiration. As if there was something sublime about the power instinct, we worship the powerful even against our will and the aura of determination and boldness seems to put an Alexander the Great or a Napoleon beyond good and evil.

A certain amount of pride is associated with every initiative and a large amount of it inspires individuals to do astonishing or outrageous deeds. Fame is the reward. People who've done great things have always sought the admiration of their fellows and remembrance by posterity, and today even the increasing number of ordinary people who write their memoirs in old age are speculating about a tiny bit of fame. The thirst for glory in the Baroque age assumed downright monstrous forms. The French king Louis XIV acknowledged that in war and government affairs he was guided solely by the desire for glory and the Prussian king Frederick the Great confessed in his memoirs that only the thirst for glory had driven him to make war against Austria. And it's precisely this aspect that makes hubris particularly hated by ordinary people.

"Pride goes before destruction and a haughty spirit before a fall" — this sentence from the Biblical Book of Proverbs has become a well-known saying, although it's probably more a pious wish than a statement; however, it certainly expresses the desperate hopes of a small nation that was repeatedly caught between the neighboring superpowers. Sections of the Old Testament are nothing but an outcry against the arrogance of the powerful, the Egyptians, Assyrians, and Babylonians, who often made short shrift of the small kingdoms of Judaea and Israel, and against the relentlessness of the great powers in any age who have complete disregard for all that is precious and sacred to ordinary people. Relief at liberation is expressed in correspondingly dramatic terms, and almost takes the form of a hymn, as for example in Isaiah after the downfall of the Babylonian king: "Sheol beneath is stirred up to meet you when you come . . . Your pomp is brought down to Sheol and the sound of your harps; maggots are the bed beneath you, and worms are your covering. How are you fallen from heaven O Day Star! . . . You said in your heart: 'I will ascend to heaven; I will raise my throne above the stars of God . . . I will ascend to the tops of the clouds and will make myself like the Most High.' But you are brought down to Sheol to the depth of the pit." Such sentences reflect the immeasurable suffering the arrogant inflict on the human race with their mighty deeds, which is why the longing for justice in many places in the Old Testament culminates in the fervent hope that God will destroy all human arrogance on Judgment Day.

In the past hubris was the special preserve of the political world. Pride and arrogance were the characteristics of the aristocracy. Dictators like Adolf Hitler, Joseph Stalin, and Pol Pot then showed us the satanical side of this deadly sin. And since then all of a sudden hubris has largely disappeared from politics — only to re-emerge, however, in the economy as well as in the vast complex of science and technology. The Napoleons of today are called Bill Gates or Mark Zuckerberg. With this, fame has largely lost its attraction. Money has taken its place, and it seems to me that it's also become the proof that man is better than God.

Considerable signs of pride, even megalomania can also be detected in the thinking of intellectuals. I remember the leader of the 1968 movement, Rudi Dutschke, saying with shining eyes in a television interview, "Today we have the possibility of liberating the entire world." You could sense his joy at being able to see the whole of life, the whole world as a project and himself as the motor in a dynamic process of almost universal dimensions, and you fluctuated, as is often the case with hubris, between being amazed at such a high level of noble-mindedness and shaking your head over his exaggerated opinion of himself.

I had a similar experience in a lecture by the philosopher Jürgen Habermas at the beginning of the 1970s in Rome. Since we could no longer speak of objective moral standards in our times, Habermas explained, these standards should be negotiated democratically. That gave me a very strange feeling. It would be the beginning of a whole new chapter in human history if somebody declared megalomania to be a general principle, if was democratically decided we could all strive to be like God. Because it's obvious that if standards are determined at our discretion, we can also revoke them at any time. Or should governments anchor morals in law? We would then have a moral police state . . . If we voted on standards, I told Habermas, it could be decided democratically that Hitler was right.

In one respect, nothing has changed by comparison with the past: monumental buildings were already the embodiment of pride and presumption in the early history of mankind and today, ironically, they are more so than ever, for it's a deadly sin to consider something impracticable and it's unthinkable not to continue with it to the end even if this is the case. It thus looks as if we've entered the epoch of construction projects beyond our control. The Elbe Philharmonic Hall in Hamburg and the airport in Berlin are the best-known examples, but they're being eclipsed by a construction project on the Finnish coast: the largest nuclear power plant in the world and possibly the most expensive ruin of all time. The incredible sum of eight billion euros has been invested in this undertaking so far, and from all I hear it's doomed to failure. This is not the only reason why it's comparable with the Tower of Babel; it will probably also fail for the same reasons as that did. The story runs as follows.

The flood has receded, the earth has been repopulated and next in Genesis we find a record of the mighty city construction projects in Mesopotamia. In the wonderfully descriptive language of the Old Testament it says, "And they had brick for stone, and bitumen for mortar. Then they said: 'Come, let us build ourselves a city and a tower with its top in the heavens and let us make a name for ourselves . . .'" They set to work and God comes to the same conclusion as he did after the Fall, that a second artificial paradise was being created: ". . . this is only the beginning; nothing that they propose to do will now be impossible for them." In other words, here a power center was emerging the likes of which had never been seen on earth before, and like all power centers it would emanate evil. God sees himself obliged to intervene but interestingly he doesn't destroy this city as he later destroys Sodom and Gomorra. Instead he abolishes the conditions that will enable this ambitious work to succeed: "They are one people, and they have all one language . . . Come, let us go down and confuse their language there, so they will not understand one another's speech."

So this is what happens. The organization of the gigantic joint project breaks down and the work on the city and the tower has to be terminated . . . And now this spectacular scene is transferred from the Orient to the coast of the Baltic Sea several millennia later, to the construction site of a massive nuclear power plant. Two of the biggest engineering companies in Europe are in charge of the implementation. Hundreds of engineers and workers have flocked here from all parts of Europe, a fantastic body of specialist knowledge is concentrated in this location, but the whole enterprise can no longer be coordinated. The common language, English, is already leading to misunderstandings at the planning level and most of the workers don't understand it at all, so there is literally a babel of languages. In addition, no one is basically responsible any more, because everyone has lost track of the proceedings and consequently everyone is planning and building without reference to anyone else, just like in Babylon.

The dimensions are too vast, the technology too complicated, and the financial loss disastrous — people have overextended themselves. And yet . . .The failure of hubris is at least spectacular. And what better symbolizes both human energy and the futility of all efforts than the Tower of Babel? The painters of the Renaissance and Baroque thus loved this theme and created impressive monuments to hubris. Feverish energy pulses through their portrayals of the building of the tower, with flames shooting from the brick kilns, grey smoke billowing out of the lime kilns and teams of horses towing stone blocks on carts to the builder's huts for preparation by an army of masons, while the architects and rulers dressed in purple lean over the plans in the foreground. And high above this scene packed with activity and radiating boundless energy rises this half-finished tower in all its splendor which is destined by God to be nothing but a ruin . . .

Of course hubris looks different today. The consequences of megalomania are rarely as spectacular as this nowadays. Every individual and every area of life are now coming rapidly but insidiously, invisibly, and inaudibly under the control of powers that today divide the divine power among themselves: business, above all the advertising industry, Internet companies, the state, secret services, biotechnology, psychiatry, etc. With the help of digital technology, everything has become possible. Every step we take can be traced, retraced, and forecast, sequencers spit out our genotype, computers our consumer behavior. We are under constant observation and well on our way to mutating from individuals to guinea pigs — helpless beings in need of improvement that can't be left alone for a second. I will only mention one example here, the attempt of psychology to take possession of our inner life.

Almost any behavior deviating from the ideal image of a well-functioning labor and consumption robot is classified as pathological, at least this is what is written in the latest issue of the *American Handbook of Psychiatry*. The most everyday forms of suffering are dramatized here and described as states requiring treatment. Someone who mourns the loss of a loved one for more than two months is disturbed according to this and such conditions must be immediately remedied with medication — the pharmaceutical industry solves all mental problems. No crucial experience can be lived out and integrated into one's life history any more, every maturing process is blocked at the outset. Everything is repairable, controllable, feasible: this is the credo of the technical world to which we are now assigned whether we want to be or not. As a result of this development, 38 percent of all Europeans suffer from neurophysiological disorders, most commonly anxiety, followed by sleeplessness and depression, according to a study by the Technical University of Dresden in 2011.

More than one third of Europeans unbalanced? I wonder whether such findings correspond at all to reality. It's probably merely the case that in this area, in the field of the human psyche, the would-be improvers of the world and the human race reign unchecked.

It used to be said that hubris ran the risk of overshooting and then turning from a constructive into a destructive force. But where there's no goal there can be no stopping. The supreme law to which we've submitted ourselves bids us carry on, continue to storm ahead, research and develop, we just mustn't stop or reflect, we should rather be happy with something that's failed, rather reconcile ourselves to threatening situations than stop. "Nothing is currently as frowned upon as skepticism about our way of life," said the writer Martin Mosebach, commenting on the incomprehensible self-satisfaction and self-confidence of the believer in progress.

Or are we in fact pursuing a goal? Might the self-abolition of the human being perhaps be a logical development of megalomania? Do we sense that the dream of people in the past of an existence beyond the oppressive reality on earth can be realized by digitalization? After all, it seems to be our dearest wish — one could almost say since Adam and Eve — to freely shape our destiny relieved of all natural and social conditions; we seem to be willing to pay any price for it. Could it be that with the transition to an entirely virtual existence we've reached our goal of being fully equal to God?

19

"The process may take several seconds" — impatience

"A stress-free Christmas" proclaimed the headline in a large German tabloid two weeks before Christmas. The article that followed filled a whole page and basically said you could save yourself all the work of preparing for Christmas because everything you needed was available on the Internet: the ideas for presents, the presents themselves, the Christmas tree (already decorated), the cookies, the festive meal, the Christmas music, and the Christmas story in St. Luke's Gospel — all from the Net. All you had to do was depress a few keys and open the front door when the bell rang and Christmas would pass by you in a flash . . . . So why celebrate Christmas at all, I thought. Then it would be better to do something else altogether with these few days. Or was the point of this "stress-free" Christmas that in this way you could do two things at the same time, for example celebrate Christmas and work at home for the firm all through the holiday? The only benefit of this festival from the Internet would then be to save time and thus gain time.

Time saved? Time gained? So is time money? We're at any rate talking about time in the same way we talk about money. We use time, we lose time, we waste time, we invest time, we gain time, and we save time. Can we own time? And does it make us happy to own time? Is time ultimately like money in this respect too — making us happy if we have none or little of it but unhappy if we have too much of it?

The next question would then be whether there's greed for time like there is for money? For this, time would have to be increased, or rather extended. But how can this be done?

It appears to be feasible. The proven way to extend time is to shorten it. In other words, shorten the time a particular process takes, such as doing the washing or preparing the Christmas meal. Now you've gained time and can immediately move on to the next thing. The less time the individual processes take, the more can be fitted into an hour, day or year. The effect of extending time by shortening it is that you can experience and achieve more in the same period of time and time goes faster. But time that goes faster is over sooner. Thus by saving time you can lose time. The more time is filled the less of it you have, because what can you do with the time you've gained? Yes, you would have time if you didn't do anything with it. But if time was only to be saved in order to do nothing, you wouldn't bother to save it at all.

The purpose of time is to cram it full, I think you will agree with me. Time must be occupied, filled. Only fully-packed time makes people happy. In other words, the less time people have, the happier they must be and the happiest people must therefore be those who have no time.

Nothing seems to be worse than having time. We're frankly at war with time. It's our greatest enemy. It's merciless, it robs us of our lives. The worst thing is to passively watch time carrying out its awful work of destroying our lives by running impassively away. So if we really do have time, the only thing that helps is a packed program, a mass of meaningful or meaningless activities, filling, planning, structuring, and managing time. In order to at least use it, or kill it if necessary so that we notice as little as possible how it's vanishing. In a breathless state we notice it least.

Waiting time is particularly awful. This time in which no wish is fulfilled and nothing's going the way we want it to, this time that just passes by unused, that simply continues unchecked to do the only thing it does, run out. No, we hate time. And would like to have more of it. Much more. It would make us happiest of all to have time. To not have to hurry, to be able to tackle things slowly, to be able to manage time as the whim takes us, to be able in part to savor it... The problem is, we don't own time. As little as we do our lives. Time is totally indifferent to us, it runs on inflexibly and all we can do is wring as much as possible out of it and cram as much as possible into it.

Time is running out on me... This used to happen at most to merchants or military commanders, today it happens to everybody. This is something new and the phenomenon that has spread through society as a result, impatience, is also relatively new. The feeling of being forced to fill time. To optimize it, as it were, in the same way as everything else is optimized. And this constraint is so strong that today we need have no qualms about ranking it before the natural driving forces. Yes, next to money, which was proclaimed as the new god two hundred years ago, we can say that there's now an equally important god: speed.

And as we have seen, this god of speed also expects us to sacrifice our reason. Our relationship to time is paradoxical and downright absurd, and as a self-deceptive maneuver basically has a profound effect on our lives. Instead of letting time come to us, we live against it like a racing driver driving against the clock. I have therefore allowed myself to add impatience as a new deadly sin. In the past too, the catalog of vices was repeatedly changed and adjusted to take account of new trends and the effects of impatience seems to me to justify this high-handedness. For example, the curious effect of feeling a degree of satisfaction over the saving of only a few minutes' time that is just as over-exaggerated as our anger over a few minutes of waiting.

In actual fact while waiting we experience a moment of truth. Because suddenly we have time, quite unexpectedly, time that can't be readily filled, and now we're suddenly aware of the hated passing of time. In this situation we feel that we've lost control over time, that we're not able to silence this life destroyer and make it disappear as usual. At such moments we become aware of our powerlessness with growing unease and realize what a childish illusion it is to believe you could gain or lose time, shorten or extend it or somehow be in control of it!

This helplessness would possibly be bearable for a short time. But waiting has a more hurtful discovery in store for us. We realize that we've been sidelined — and nobody cares two hoots about it. We've been left standing, cast aside, and the world carries on turning without us. It's not just that we're by no means the center of the world that we think we are, but that at this moment we're apparently superfluous! It's the ultimate mortification for the narcissist. It's not about the few minutes or hours that are gained or lost. We lose our temper when waiting, because we experience the greatest imaginable humiliation. And the euphoria we feel when we gain time is because our illusion that we can control time is strengthened. An evidently necessary illusion.

And so as soon as we have time we start to shorten it and kill it. One study found that the average German doesn't even wait five minutes if the person they're expecting isn't punctual. We see that young people aren't 30 seconds on public transport before they take out their smart phones — older people wait a little longer. And in my experience not even five seconds' waiting are considered reasonable. When ordering an airline ticket on the Internet I read the following sentence during a search process: "Please be patient, the process may take several seconds." Several seconds' free time, empty time, thus lost time? This deserves an apology.

Those who succumb to the tempo of our time suffer first of all themselves, because a constant increase in activity means always being in a rush. We would only have time if we did nothing or very little with it, but this is unthinkable. Several times a day we're faced with the decision as to whether we let something go or call a halt. Accept or do something about it. Resign ourselves or rebel. Let things happen or take matters into our own hands. And together with hubris, rationality whispers in our ear every time: You can do better! Take your fate into your own hands and intervene, control, speed things up! Our life is the most precious asset we have, so we mustn't leave it unattended for a moment. . . .

Those who are impatient and greedy for time therefore specialize in forcing things along, which is often masked as parental care or sacrificing themselves for some purpose. The obsession with optimization affects sons and daughters before they are out of infancy. The foundation stone for their future career has to be laid in kindergarten and when they come home with their first low grade, private tutors are immediately summoned. The problems of young people are increasingly being tackled with the kind immediate measures and programs that are common in the working world and politics, and corresponding results are expected. And in this way impatience is passed on — the first disappointment is sufficient reason to break up with the new girlfriend and a person who hasn't got in contact after a few days is dropped. The impatient don't do justice to others, have no understanding for them, and don't accept them as independent, idiosyncratic individuals.

For in order to understand another person one must listen. Patiently spend time with him or her and listen. It's a time-consuming process. The world-famous physicist and financial expert Emanuel Derman once described in a newspaper article how much willpower was needed in order to respond to someone and how much one had to hold back. If I want to understand a person, he said, I must be prepared to be silent and neither express criticism nor agreement but simply listen. Sometimes it's even necessary to listen patiently to the most ridiculous nonsense without raising one's eyebrows. It's not a matter of finding out the opinions of the other person, but of gaining access to his or her innermost being, and to achieve that it's necessary to let the other person act on you. I think it's good to remind ourselves of this occasionally. Taking others seriously requires time and nerves.

Listen patiently, observe patiently, don't stop anyone in their tracks, don't act the know-all or comment disparagingly . . . Nowadays you don't experience this very often. What is much more common is the millionfold cry of indignation on the Internet and in the media. A statement only has to contain something objectionable for the cursory listener for the cartel of moral guardians to be aroused and expect the worst. What if it was neither said nor meant this way? A general public in a state of permanent alarm doesn't take the time to listen carefully. In a climate of nervous irritability, understanding isn't very popular. Which leads us to a further very German reason for impatience: dogmatism. Perfectionism, also in the moral sense.

Here in Rome serenity reigns. In spite of the chaos on the roads, drivers don't get upset. People are in any case easily satisfied with second best, perfection isn't expected, and the outraged cry, "But that's impossible, he can't do that!" is never heard. In Germany, however, people are quick to find intolerable what others elsewhere consider quite acceptable and then it's *tabula rasa*. Reorganize everything! Change the whole system, or we quit! Quit the ADAC, for example, in droves because after 50 years some improper practices have crept in . . . A society is much more relaxed if everyone doesn't always have to take up a stance . . . and the root of evil is sometimes also allowed to stay in the ground.

It seems to me that impatience is ultimately bred of pessimism. One is unable to believe things will end well, one always expects the worst. Impatient people are allergic to mistakes and breakdowns and only their own intervention releases them from the torture of witnessing certain failure. For this reason they can't rely on anything, can't let things take their course or develop. With them, plans and programs have replaced everything that perhaps under other circumstances would be the normal run of things, the natural development — or possibly an adventure. I feel that this urge to control is born of the same pessimism as the dark visions of the future portrayed by artists and intellectuals.

Must impatience therefore be considered evil? Not necessarily. Impatience is basically no more evil than all the previous deadly sins. Like hubris it can be a positive force, a force for changing intolerable conditions, a force of opposition against the unreasonable. But when it gets the upper hand, when it has already become a basic attitude, it becomes a plague. What has always been valid as a law of life, that to do something well takes time, is sacrificed to this absurd greed for time. Or in the words of an African saying: "Grass doesn't grow any faster if you pull at it with your teeth."

20

An invigorating feeling — anger

Anger. Rage. So many pictures come to mind. Teenage hooligans supporting two opposing teams who attack one another vociferously after a game. Masked Molotov cocktail-throwing anarchists who fought street battles with the police in Berlin. Agitated crowds at a demonstration on Cairo's Tahir Square. The outbursts of Hitler's supreme judge Roland Freisler at the People's Court. The revenge killing of two Muslims who hacked a British soldier to pieces with a machete and hatchet on a London street in broad daylight. Moses who shattered the tablets of the covenant in a fit of righteous anger at the sight of the golden calf. The frenzied attacker who enters a school during teaching hours and shoots at teachers and students. And a personal memory: a memorial on the piazza of a small town in northern Italy. On two bronze panels, the sculptor Carlo Santachiara has depicted war and peace. One shows cultivated fields and gardens in a rolling landscape. The order, diligence, peace, and happiness in this scene are literally palpable, while the other panel depicts armored horsemen plunging ahead, waves of combatants, and nations in an uproar, to quote the Old Testament. Why do we spend longer looking at the presentation of war than at that of peace? Because war stirs us up? Because the soul wants to be stirred up?

In any case we're quick to get excited, with few exceptions. It doesn't have to be rage right away, or righteous anger, there are a lot of preliminary stages and practically anything can put us in a momentary rage — a door slamming, loud music in the neighborhood, a slow driver in the fast lane. The ego has a low fuse and the humiliating experience of one's own powerlessness leads it to erupt violently much too violently, even for minor reasons. To then lose control of oneself may be described as a blissful state, even if it only results in imprecations. What I find really amazing, however, is something else: the widespread desire to be offended.

When I think back to my youth, I remember conversations in my family circle where all those who were absent were judged mercilessly. I also think of many other people I've met who sieve through their lives in the hope of finding a slight which justifies being outraged. Never mind how far-fetched, it's taken for granted the intention was malicious, as if the idea of being the target of malice were irresistible. Evidently these individuals want at all costs to get excited about something. Evidently in such cases anger has to be continuously refueled. But why? For what purpose?

I suspect that it's in order to feel strong and in the right. Only anger entitles such people, positively authorizes them to act decisively and assume a morally justified power position that gives them the pleasant feeling of superiority. Anger makes them courageous. Rage makes them strong. So they assume the other person set out to offend in order to draw energy from the apparently justified outrage, which is why nothing is worse than people who mean well by them. A world where no offense is given leaves them powerless; it doesn't allow them to raise themselves to a position of strength. In other words: the fly in the ointment is pure soul food, and even the slightest animosity has a stimulating effect on people who are otherwise unable to assert themselves. And there are many of them, an enormous number. In particular where they can show their true colors without having to show their face: on the Internet.

What shows up here in numerous commentaries is a merciless judgment of others born of narrow-mindedness. Internet forums are unrivaled for self-righteous sarcasm and a tone ranging from arrogance to pure contempt, and the anonymity favors a lack of self-control which was formerly the characteristic of the hostile crowd, the lynch mob. These outpourings are nevertheless revealing — you can sense how happy it makes people to lose control over themselves and indulge in unchecked hatred of everyone who thinks or feels differently. It's certainly no longer possible to speak of impatience here, but rather of an angry basic mood and a kind of ruthless close combat morality, which is rampant everywhere interpersonal relationships mainly take place via the Internet or cell phone. It almost looks as if more and more people, especially youngsters, are discovering rage and hate as a source of energy for themselves. And what has remained of their conscience is drowned by the inner howl of triumph after they've abundantly demonstrated their superiority, primarily over weaker individuals.

It's probably more difficult to set oneself limits with anger than with any other deadly sin. First, because anger often suddenly overcomes you and doesn't creep up on you like other deadly sins until it one day becomes a character trait, and because the force of the outbreak also affects the body — your heart rate increases, your blood pressure rises, and your focus narrows. Second, because anger can become aimless rage if it doesn't soon subside and rage in the long run can become a mixture of resentment, rancor, and hate which can ignite like an explosive gas at any time — in this state anybody who's in my way can become an enemy and be treated as such. A society which emphasizes the liberation of urges and rejects religious and social norms as unwanted meddling in one's private life and whose members probably have the battle cry of the 1968 generation in their ears — "Destroy what destroys you!" is fertile ground for anger and rage. Although anger isn't limited to our latitudes. From what ethnologists have discovered, it may be considered the only truly universal deadly sin.

Anger — or in the wider sense aggression — is something elemental. Unlike envy, greed, and narcissism it occurs in all the cultures of the world and can be observed in people everywhere from a very young age. However, also by contrast with all other vices, there's something curious about anger: a tiny moment of hesitation at the outset, when the individual is beginning to get angry but hasn't yet lost control. For a few seconds you feel that the die hasn't yet been cast and that a decision in favor of reason and self-control is still possible. If this moment isn't used, then all is lost. But there is this last barrier and you don't necessarily automatically pitch a fit – even if it looks more and more like this. Young people in particular don't seem to notice an inhibition threshold any more, as if this last barrier had disappeared, as if the possibility of deciding against the intoxicating rush of energy supplied by anger was no longer worth considering.

Instead of listing all the examples of vandalism, violence, and lack of inhibition, I would like to cite an interview with the chief of police of Tokyo. In 2013, the crimes committed in the entire Japanese subway network amounted to 350 cases of pickpocketing. In German subways in the same year there had been 2,300 serious cases of violence including several cases of homicide. When asked for the reason for this discrepancy, the chief of police had only one explanation. Without hesitating he said drily, "We bring up our children to be respectful and courteous."

We're addicted to anger. People with a cool temperament, who have themselves well under control, may perhaps enjoy our respect but not necessarily our sympathy. Getting angry is human, and getting angry together with others is even better. In addition, anger and outrage provide a dramatic touch that some people are sorely missing in their lives. And finally the majority of us are grateful for anger, rage, and violence as long as it doesn't come too close, so when it's in the form of movies, novels, and video games. Everything that was said in the second chapter about the dramatic dimension of evil primarily refers to the fruits of anger and the elementary, destructive force with which the unleashed energies invade our lives. The blazing fury of the righteous, the revenge of the humiliated person, the bitter family feud, the deadly fraternal strife, all these belong on the stage, on the screen, between book covers, for no deadly sin offers such morbid attractions as anger, and human beings want to be stirred up. Although we all have very different reactions when we witness anger.

Angry people can make themselves look as ridiculous as Rumpelstiltskin when the cause of their outburst is ridiculous. They can arouse disgust when they have struck indiscriminately in cold, blind fury. But they can also achieve an intimidating and awe-inspiring effect when they have a very good reason for their outburst. Loudly and dramatically voiced anger should shake others awake and show how much harm or injustice has been done; the rebel can get people onto his or her side and usually be sure of our sympathy. Anger therefore often has a theatrical component. Moses, for example, who after his return found the people dancing around the golden calf, was so enraged he shattered the tablets of the covenant dictated to him personally by God — his anger was undoubtedly authentic but didn't the outrageous gesture of shattering the tablets have an intentionally dramatic effect? Or Jesus, who got angry over the dealers in the temple, made a whip out of cords and assaulted the sellers and money changers — his indignation was undoubtedly real but doesn't this scene look deliberately staged? The Spaniard Baltasar Gracián (1601-58), who with his *Hand Oracle* wrote the most perceptive book about worldly wisdom, even advises using anger on purpose in public to emphasize one's point of view beyond all argument. However, he believes that it's the greatest stupidity of all to allow oneself to be carried away by one's anger.

Just as greed and hubris need attributes, visible signs that glorify the greedy and megalomaniac, so anger has also acquired a certain visual identity: that of the American-style motorbike rockers. The attitude and equipment of biker gangs such as Hell's Angels conjures up the image of anger, rage, contempt, and brutality, and reflects in every detail the belief in the right of the stronger; you could actually say that they give the underlying aggressiveness of our time a representative face. In such a milieu, extreme acts of violence are honored with special awards and the popularity of these groups is in my view one of the most obvious crisis symptoms.

An interesting aspect of these biker gangs is the absence of women. It's a masculine world and in the history of anger women do indeed play a minor role. Recently they've been catching up and in the meantime in movies and in the real world there are female figures who no longer differ in their ruthless brutality from men — at most these women are cooler and more objective than violent male criminals, less impetuous as it were. But still women are looked on more as having a calming effect when men get angry. I found an unexpected reference to the traditional role of women as mediators in the Edda, the collection of Scandinavian mythological stories. Even during the extravagant feasts of the Germanic gods in Valhalla one can read that Freya and other goddesses boldly intervened to prevent the worst when the male gods in their drunkenness clashed with each other and reached for their swords. They also, incidentally, proved themselves to be more than competent at this by no means an easy task . . .

Anger is masculine and is intended to be seen as a show of force. "Only slaves never get angry," Aristotle said. Anger is almost always primarily caused by a desperate feeling of powerlessness, a sense of not being heard, not being understood, and being ignored, in short it's the outcome of being unable to assert oneself otherwise. The most horrific outbreaks of hate and vengeance are based on this feeling of powerlessness, insofar as they can be explained at all — the mass murder of 77 young people whom the Norwegian Anders Breivik gunned down indiscriminately on a vacation island in 2011, and the genocide in Rwanda in 1994, when approximately one million Tutsi were killed. The same feeling of powerlessness probably also nourishes the mood of anger and violence that is expressed in the rising incidents of vandalism and the increasingly frequent attacks on referees at youth games or the upsurge in the number of brutal attacks on police, to name just a few examples.

The most harrowing effect of anger is that its consequences are mostly irreparable. Everyone who's got carried away and written an angry letter has experienced that in the blink of an eye so much damage has been done that it can never be made good. For this reason alone a society should consider whether it wants to continue to demonize all curbing of our instincts — and whether freedom has really been gained when all moral control instances disappear. In this context I remember Simeon and Levi, the two sons of the patriarch Jacob, who were responsible for the previously mentioned carnage at Shechem.

It looked as if Jacob accepted the desecration of their sister as an excuse. Jacob only seemed to be criticizing them for rashness and shortsightedness. The slaughter among the population of Shechem wasn't reprehensible to him according to this. And then much later when Jacob was on his deathbed he summoned his sons, praised their virtues and merits and predicted their future, only to lose his temper on hearing the names of Simeon and Levi. "Weapons of violence are their swords!" he exclaimed. "For in their anger they killed men . . . Cursed be their anger, for it is fierce, and their wrath, for it is cruel! I will . . . scatter them in Israel." So what we as readers felt was an outrageous piece of wickedness, was seen in the same way by Jacob after all, and he finally meted out punishment.

21

Open to anything — faithlessness

Sometimes in old movies you hear the words "I'll wait for you," when two people say goodbye to one another — when the lover goes to war, or the beloved goes on board an ocean liner. "I'll wait for you," they say to each other — and they do indeed wait.

Do you still hear these words today? Or don't you rather ask yourself in these demoralized times how people could bear it in the past, only being connected in their thoughts, only now and then getting a letter as a sign of life, but otherwise having nothing in their hands, while in their hearts there was only longing and the courage to remain faithful? I still treasure some letters I have in my possession that my father wrote to my mother from Crete during the war. They had married only shortly before and lost sight of each other for almost seven years — during this time my father came home on leave only twice, otherwise they wrote to each other, but their love didn't suffer as a result. I remember very clearly how they embraced each other on my father's return. Were people's hearts in the past stronger and bolder or more humble and undemanding? They were at any rate less compromising. "I wanted this man or no one. I knew he was the right person and he was," said an elderly actress whose name I've forgotten in an interview — and 60 years lay between the first feeling of certainty and the second. Those who are so sure will wait. There is nothing better they can do, because nothing better could happen to them ...

Was there a lot of idealization in the past? Possibly. But if a realistic view leads to the loss of something as great as fidelity, if something as contemptuous as disloyalty becomes increasingly socially acceptable, then I prefer the idealistic view.

Of course faithlessness isn't on the classic list of deadly sins any more than impatience is. But on the one hand there is a connection between the two and on the other hand disloyalty is associated with falseness and faintheartedness and in my opinion merits a chapter of its own. And its inclusion among the deadly sins is mainly because of what I've been finding for a long time, also in the context of my order: people don't want to commit themselves. Many no longer say vows, which also in fact seem anachronistic in an age that demands full flexibility and mobility. Under these circumstances, loyalty denotes a lack of enterprise, because who wants to miss an opportunity for economic and social advancement? Who wants to miss an experience? And who wants to be labelled as not being open to anything?

Open to anything . . . Picture this literally and people resemble sieves; everything that pours over them flows away immediately. They get nothing out of anything and their environment gets nothing from them. In the past, the idea of introducing "temporary monasticism" was floated in our order as a solution to the lack of new intake in our European and American monasteries. I had reservations. Like marriage, monasticism requires you to concentrate all your strength on an ideal. It doesn't work as a temporary experiment, because it then loses its meaning, it's a lifetime's work.

However, it's always been hard to undertake a lifelong obligation. If it's even harder today, this could be because people now avoid subjecting themselves to such a test if it doesn't involve their career, money or social advancement. When it involves a quite different, much greater but distant happiness, which requires staying power and persistent effort. Or, in everyday terms, when it's the test everyday life imposes on the love relationship of every couple and every joint living arrangement, as this also requires not only great perseverance but also a high degree of reliability.

To stand by a person, or a conviction. To give your word and keep it. To be loyal. Why should you do that at all? Why not find fulfillment on your own and use the others as a stepping-stone or a springboard? Here a minor betrayal of your own ideals, there a minor betrayal of a friend, and that's all it takes to get you playing golf with the right people in the right club — so why not?

Because every human relationship is based on trust. The guilelessness, naturalness, and good faith that are the unique qualities of an intimate relationship are only possible through trust. Trust is the basis of a community's cohesion and the disloyal person undermines it. Such a person has the diabolical power of turning trust into mistrust and inflicting the deepest emotional wounds. Faithlessness and betrayal are therefore not dismissed as pardonable carelessness and usually everybody knows this. So how come they nevertheless repeatedly occur?

I think every traitor is motivated by the belief that in the interest of personal advantage, nothing is sacred. With such narcissistic thinking, the prospect of a new, greater happiness invalidates previous ties and obligations. This is also called unscrupulousness and of course you can go a long way with this in business life. Everywhere else, however, there is nothing that degrades a person in the eyes of others as much as the betrayal, abuse, and exploitation of fellow human beings, the breach of trust. It's not without reason that in certain organizations betrayal is considered a particularly serious offense and punished very severely. It involves at least the loss of honor and the disloyal person must reckon with a milder form of contempt at least in his or her circle of friends and acquaintances. This is about something fundamental, about a basic human need. The longing for connectedness. This is the sacred thing that betrayers sin against in order to promote their own interests, this is what they wantonly desecrate.

I believe that every human being intuitively perceives the division and fragmentation, discord and strife that persists on earth as an unnatural situation. As something that is as alien to us as evil. Any moral sensitivity, any serious idea of happiness is probably based on the feeling that we are living under distorted conditions that are essentially foreign to us. And both the moral sensitivity and the idea of happiness are probably derived from the certainty that it doesn't have to be like this and the world was originally intended to be different. This certainty is mysterious, irrational; there is no evidence for it in reality and there is more evidence for considering discord and fragmentation to be the natural, obvious condition of human beings. Nevertheless, what is probably the deepest, most primary human longing cannot be silenced: the longing to overcome all divisions and achieve an all-encompassing connectedness.

Connectedness with our neighbors, and basically with all human beings, and loyalty to those who are close to us is inspired in exactly the same way as the hospitality and kindness extended to strangers in a foreign land. But we are also motivated to connect with an even greater reality, with nature, with everything that exists — this finds expression in the love of nature and the respect for creation. And finally we are motivated to connect with a reality which goes beyond all sensually experienced reality — to connect with God, to whom the religions point the way. The highest form of this connectedness is the mystic union with God.

There is evidence that the promise of connectedness is as irresistible as ever — even if you don't take it as far as I've just done. The most banal, mundane but no less conclusive evidence is provided by digital technology. Those who are constantly on their cell or smart phones, who voluntarily spend days and nights at the computer, are doing it in the expectation of participating in the greatest conceivable reality and experiencing all-embracing connectedness. Seen in this light, the rampant computer and cell phone addiction is nothing more than an attempt to experience with the inadequate media of technology something only religion used to offer. All these technical devices are now being used as if they had taken root and ceased to be lifeless objects — they are turning into something that is alive, has a soul and is thus akin to religious forms of communication with the divine. While technology doesn't keep its promises — it isolates and destroys what it claims to provide — the desire for connectedness is evidently ineradicable.

Connectedness with everything around us is what it's all been about from the beginning, more or less since Adam and Eve. Connectedness and its endangerment by the irresponsible use human beings make of their freedom is the subject of the fall of the human race, of the Bible as a whole and what people have made of it ever since — whether they expose this original scandal to ridicule through jokes and humor and thus make it bearable, play it down with cynicism, and thus declare it irrelevant, or portray it with theological and philosophical seriousness in all its shocking drama and derive from it an ongoing task for humanity.

To return now finally to evil in general, it could be said that any assault on this connectedness in the broadest sense is wicked. And all those who opt for the adversarial in situations where connectedness is involved in its most basic form ally themselves with evil. This can happen in the most ordinary everyday situation — the office intrigue that robs a handful of people of their work satisfaction is as morally reprehensible as the machinations of Wall Street, if significantly less dangerous.

What I have been trying to clarify in this book is what we must all constantly clarify for ourselves anew: the question of when it is time for our conscience to go into action. It certainly helps to know something about the origins and manifestations of evil. Ultimately, however, it will depend more on our remaining sufficiently aware and being fundamentally ready to respond to our neighbors' needs, troubles, and hopes.

Bibliography

p. 1: On the flood in the Old Testament: Genesis 7:1-24; 8:1-22.

p. 1: On the flood in Greek mythology: Die schönsten Sagen des klassischen Altertums, Sigbert Mohn Verlag, p. 26.

p. 9: On the vampire of Düsseldorf: Hanno Parmentier, *Der Würger von Düsseldorf*, Sutton Verlag, 2013.

p. 12: On the relapse of Alipius: *Augustinus, Bekenntnisse*, VMA-Verlag, pp. 134-35.

p. 28: On the temptation of Jesus: Matthew 4:1-11.

p. 31: On the degree of planning by criminals: Claudia Brockmann, *Warum Menschen töten*, ullstein extra, 2013, p. 46.

p. 32: On the prodigal son: Luke 15:11-32.

p. 36: On guilt among the early Israelites: Jeremiah 2:23-24, 34-35.

p. 36: On the bloodbath in Shechem: Genesis 34:1-31.

p. 42: On Ezekiel: Ezekiel 18:2, 18-19.

p. 53: On aggression in children: Irenäus von Eibl-Eibelsfeld, *Aggression*, dtv Wissenschaft, 1982, p. 122ff.

p. 56: On the Fall of Man: Genesis 2:7-25; 3:1-24.

p. 64: (see also p.) On Cain and Abel: Genesis 4:1-12.

p. 82: On pessimistic visions of the future: Martin Mosebach, *Als das Reisen noch geholfen hat*, Hanser Verlag, 2011, p. 331.

p. 85: On moral over-zealousness: Friedrich Siegburg, *Robespierre*, DVA, 1958, p. 34.

p. 85: On moral over-zealousness: M. Agejew, *Roman mit Kokain*, Manesse Verlag, 2012, p. 202ff.

p. 100: On post-humans: Die Zeit, 8.5.2013, Hirnschrittmacher für alle! Interview with the philospher Stefan Lorenz Sorgner

p. 101: On post-humans: Welt am Sonntag, 16.3.2014, Ich bin ein Avatar, holt mich hier raus! By Klja Riechert

p. 108: On wealth: Ecclesiastes 5:9-14.

p. 109: On wealth: Ecclesiastes 10:19.

p. 110: On wealth: Luke 18:25.

p. 110: On greed in the New Testament, 1 Timothy 6:7-10.

p. 111: On greed in Antwerp: Lust und Laster – Die 7 Todsünden von DürerbisNaumann, Kunst Museum, Bern, 2011, p. 201.

p. 117: On egoism: Frank Schirrmacher, *Ego : Das Spiel des Lebens*, Karl Blessing Verlag, 2013.

p. 121: On Evagrius Ponticus: *Evagrius Ponticus, Die große Widerrede*, Vier Türme Verlag, 2012.

p. 132: On the fable of the envious person: Johannes von Salisbury, Policraticus, VII.24.

p. 141: On belongings in the monastery: *Die Benediktregel*, Benziger Verlag, 1982, chapter 33.

p. 155: On imperiousness: Egon Friedell, *Kulturgeschichte der Neuzeit*, Diogenes Verlag, 2009, p. 1551.

p. 158: On pride: Proverbs 16:18.

p. 159: On the downfall of the king of Babylon: Isaiah 14:9-15.

p. 161: On the building of the Tower of Babel: Genesis 11:1-9.

p. 176: On deliberate outbreaks of anger; Baltasar Gracián, *Handorakel und Kunst der Weltklugheit*, Schünemann Verlag, 1982, § 155.

p. 178: On the cursing of Simeon and Levi: Genesis 49:5-7.

Illustrations: Abstract paintings by Dr Ingrid Kerky: Evil, The Fall, Envy, Greed, Narcissism, Hubris, Anger, Faithlessness (open to anything).